Bergen County
Voices from the
AMERICAN
REVOLUTION

Bergen County
Voices from the
AMERICAN
REVOLUTION

Soldiers and Residents in Their Own Words

TODD W. BRAISTED

Charleston | London

THE
History
PRESS

Published by The History Press
Charleston, SC 29403
www.historypress.net

Front cover: Guns of the re-created Lamb's and Mott's Artillery Companies fire over the Hackensack River at Historic New Bridge Landing during the 2001 Retreat event. *Courtesy of Janet Strom.*

First published 2012

Manufactured in the United States

ISBN 978.1.60949.836.8

Library of Congress CIP data applied for.

CONTENTS

CONTENTS

Justus Earle at age seventy-one. Earle was a Loyalist from Hackensack Township and served as an officer in the Fourth Battalion, New Jersey Volunteers. This watercolor and ink on vellum was painted by Thomas MacDonald in Earle's postwar home of New Brunswick, Canada. *Courtesy of the New Brunswick Museum, Saint John, N.B. Accession 2006.1.*

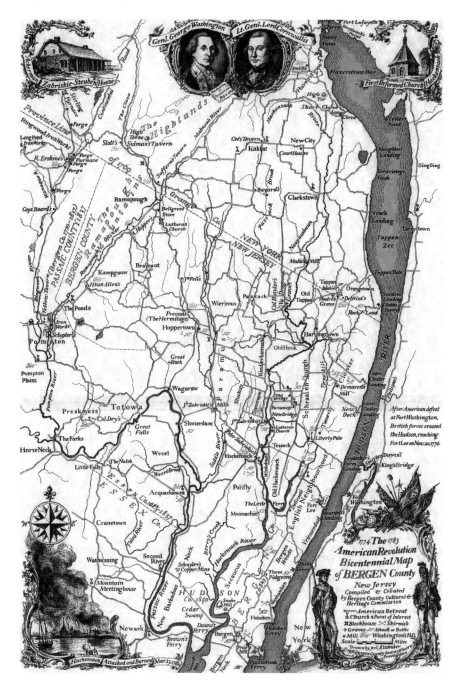

1976 map of Revolutionary War incidents in Bergen County. *Courtesy of Bergen County Division of Cultural and History Affairs.*

INTRODUCTION

Bergen County, tucked into the northeast corner of New Jersey, saw as much of the American Revolution on its doorstep as any other locale in North America. For seven years, the main British Army occupied New York City and its environs, including a part of Bergen County, at Paulus Hook, modern Jersey City. Geographically speaking, Bergen County of the eighteenth century was much larger than the Bergen County of today, encompassing all of what is now Hudson County and a large part of Passaic County, both of which were created in the nineteenth century. It was bordered on the east by the Hudson River, to the south by Newark Bay and Staten Island, to the west by the Passaic River and New York State to the north.

European settlement in the county had commenced some 130 years before the war and included a wide range of nationalities, including Dutch, English, Irish, Scottish, German, French, Danish and Polish. Joined to a not inconsiderable number of free and enslaved African American residents, the residents of Bergen County formed a unique culture and population, one that would become a microcosm for modern America.

As opposed to the seventy towns, boroughs, villages and cities that make up Bergen County today, only seven townships existed when the Revolution commenced: Bergen, Hackensack, New Barbadoes, Franklin, Saddle River, Harrington and New Barbadoes. Within these townships, settlements and towns grew up, such as Hackensack, Teaneck, Paramus and Closter, names familiar to residents today. Other villages, such as Hoppertown,

Schraalenburgh, Slotterdam and English Neighborhood, would give way to more modern names during the "borough craze" of the 1890s. No area of the county, however, would escape the effects of the Revolution.

When the Revolution broke out, Bergen County would not have been confused with cities where the Sons of Liberty held sway. The inhabitants of Bergen were deeply divided in their political views, for a variety of reasons. The people had grown prosperous under the British government, which would include New Jersey's last Royal Governor, William Franklin. The governor's legacy in the county would be secured when a newly created township was named after him in 1771. After Franklin's arrest in June 1776 by the new revolutionary state government, he was transported under armed guard to prison in Connecticut. Upon learning that the guard, with Franklin, had stopped to spend the night in Hackensack, Washington hastened them on their way, cautioning their commander that "delays are Dangerous." Franklin's replacement, the state's first governor, William Livingston, proclaimed to George Washington in 1777 "that the most northern County of the State is almost totally disaffected." All this led to a situation of civil war, not just amongst neighbors, but within families themselves.

The people presented in this work, while often neighbors or family, had very different experiences despite their common ties of culture, history and geography. When a person such as a George Hameon went off to war for the British, he had to serve for the duration of the war, eating a diet of salt beef or pork, bread, sauerkraut, oatmeal, peas, spruce beer and rum. He received a new uniform with either a red or green coat each year, had to adhere to military discipline and was liable for military service anywhere in America, for the small sum of six pence a day.

His counterpart in the fight, a Peter Van Allen, for instance, served in no standing army for Washington. The militia, unlike regularly enlisted soldiers, served for but one month at a time, generally in three or four "tours" a year. Unlike a Continental (or Provincial) soldier, the militia generally served close to home and usually in small bodies, keeping guard, patrolling the roads and intercepting the many inhabitants who did clandestine commerce with the enemy. Known as "London Traders," residents of both political persuasions found trading their produce, cattle and small finished goods for British gold or imported items more lucrative than taking depreciated paper currency from the state or Continental authorities. Both Hameon and Van Allen would have used the same or similar weapons, generally a .75-caliber smoothbore flintlock musket of British manufacture, with the

Field piece at Fort Lee Historic Park. *Courtesy of Todd W. Braisted.*

Loyalist soldier being issued his ammunition, while his counterpart would generally be responsible for providing his own.

Some people got to experience both situations, such as George Van Buskirk, who served for a year in the Continental army (the maximum term of enlistment at that time) and then the remainder of the war in the militia. Some militia were used to flesh out the Continental units to full strength for short periods, such as Harman Blauvelt. Blauvelt was one of many of these short timers (known as "levies") who expanded the Continental army in 1780 for a possible attack on British-held New York City. Not an inconsiderable number viewed the fight firsthand from both sides. Enlistment of deserters and prisoners of war, by both sides, was a common occurrence. James Kent, a militiaman taken prisoner on March 23, 1780, while serving at Hackensack, chose to serve with his Bergen neighbors under Abraham Van Buskirk in the New Jersey Volunteers rather than sit in prison and await exchange. He used the opportunity to later desert back home and resume service in the militia. Times were indeed confusing for many of these young soldiers.

Years of hostilities had led to massive damage and upheaval within the county and community. For many of the supporters of Congress, their homes had been plundered or burned, their crops and livestock appropriated (by both sides) and lives interrupted. For the Loyalists who supported King George, scores of properties had been confiscated by the state and sold at auction, with all of the owner's worldly goods. The courts had likewise convicted them, mostly in absentia, of high treason against the state, thereby proscribing and banishing them, never to legally return. Their futures lay mostly in the remainder of British North America, what are today the maritime provinces of Canada.

Their recognition and compensation for their service and losses would be a long time coming, particularly for Washington's veterans. While the state started the process of compensating its citizens for property losses before the war had even ended, the United States itself would not be so moved for decades. The first pension act, passed in 1818 and modified two years later, only provided for destitute officers and soldiers of the Continental army. It was not until 1832, a date at which most veterans were near or over seventy years of age, that all land and sea veterans were eligible, provided they had served a minimal amount of time and could offer some reasonable evidence of their activities in the war. As they passed on, this law was revised to allow pensions for their widows and families as well. While minimal in nature, these monetary awards provided some financial relief in an era before social safety nets.

For those who had retained their allegiance to King George, parliament passed an act in 1783 designed for their relief. Those who could prove losses to their personal property, profession or service could apply to commissioners appointed to evaluate their claims and award compensation. The main caveat was that the losses needed to be proved by documentary evidence, usually in the form of deeds, notarized legal documents concerning confiscation, appraisals, wills, etc. Needless to say, most Loyalists left their homes during the war without their paperwork, and there was little to no chance of obtaining it afterward. Worse, the claimants only had until March 1784 to submit their claims in London, either personally or by people acting as their attorneys. Coming at a time when most Loyalists were preoccupied in the attempt to carve out a new life for themselves in the wilds of Nova Scotia, it provided just one more logistical and financial hardship on people who had but little means. Only during the time of Queen Victoria did the new province of New Brunswick offer pensions to "Old Soldiers of the Revolution."

Bergen County, then as now, is a place of many cultures. This tablet in Dutch commemorates the building of the North Church in Schraalenburgh, now Dumont. *Courtesy of Todd W. Braisted.*

These aged veterans, and their widows, were the last remnants of Bergen County's Loyalist force.

These pension applications and compensation claims allow the actual participants of those momentous times to speak to us today. While historians may organize, analyze and verify the facts of the past, they cannot bring the emotional firsthand experiences that the participants themselves can relate. Their deeds and actions remain with us today, through the old stone homes that have survived over 225 years intact, to the battlefields that dot the landscape, the headstones scattered in the church yards and their proud descendents today, residents of two great countries, separated by the tumultuous war that separated their ancestors forever.

While the original documents are compelling reading, they do not always read easily for a modern audience. For the sake of readability and uniformity, the documents have been in part corrected in their spelling, grammar, capitalizations and abbreviations, without notice. You will still come across some odd fragments, capitalizations etc. that will give some flavor of the original documents. It should be noted that many of the U.S. pension applications were not written by the applicants themselves but rather by a clerk in open court, almost certainly in front of many other veterans there for the like reason. The dates written on the documents bear this out. Those occasions would have made for an incredible oral history of the war for the younger residents in attendance at the courts on those days. For the veterans themselves, in an age before associations such as the American Legion and VFW, it must have been a time of great pride and reflection, meeting and chatting with old comrades, reliving the shared hardships of the "Times that Tried Men's Souls."

The inspiration for this work was John Dann's wonderful *The Revolution Remembered: Eyewitness Accounts of the War for Independence*. Mr. Dann's presentation of U.S. pension applications awoke me to the possibility of using them as a vehicle to tell great stories and provide little known or unknown anecdotes that would otherwise be lost to history. I would like to thank the staff of the David Library of the American Revolution and Kathie Ludwig, in particular, for all their assistance over the years in accumulating the material for this book. Three very good friends were also invaluable in sharing their knowledge and wisdom, namely Don Hagist, for his suggestions, support and encouragement in writing; Lieutenant Colonel Don Londahl-Smidt, the premier military historian of the American Revolution; and Bergen County Historical Society past president Kevin Wright, whose knowledge of the county is absolutely unsurpassed. Deborah Powell and, indeed, all the members of the Bergen County Historical Society have been extremely generous in their support and assistance. Thanks as well to all the members of the living history community and Fort Lee Historic Park for educating so many in the life and times of the American Revolution, and who have assisted in the undertaking of this work. Thanks to my editor Whitney Tarella at The History Press for her advice, suggestions and sincere support. And finally to my wife, Susan, whose constant encouragement in this work was both needed and most appreciated.

CHAPTER 1

JOHN ALDINGTON

English Neighborhood

*J*ohn Aldington left England in 1768 to make his fortune in the New World, settling in English Neighborhood with the intention of becoming a brewer. Breweries were common in New York City at the time, but his would have been Bergen County's first such establishment. The brewing process effectively killed bacteria in the water, making the resulting product a desired part of the everyday diet and making the provider of such beverages well-to-do at the same time. The location of his brew house is not known, but his mentioning it being converted into a storehouse by the Continental army and the availability of a water carriage to New York strongly suggests it abutted the land of Fort Lee. The war putting an end to his brewing plans, Aldington joined the British prior to their arrival in New Jersey, instead assisting the Royal Navy ships then making the dangerous passages up and down the Hudson, passing between the guns of Fort Lee and its sister post across the river, Fort Washington. When it came time for Lord Cornwallis to cross the Hudson and take Fort Lee, Aldington was one of his three principal guides. For his services, Aldington was commissioned a captain in May 1777 in the corps of Guides and Pioneers, a relatively small corps with whom he would serve the remainder of the war, being promoted to major commandant in 1782. The unit would serve in detachment strength in almost every theater of the conflict, enabling the brewer turned soldier to take part in the taking of Philadelphia and Charleston, the relief of Newport and William Tryon's 1777 excursion to Connecticut. The Guides and Pioneers were likewise with Cornwallis on his 1778 Grand Forage in Bergen County, enabling Aldington to visit what had remained of his home, which would shortly thereafter be confiscated by the State of New Jersey for his having joined the British. His claim for compensation is in the United Kingdom's National Archives, AO 13/108/1-7.

That your Memorialist hath been in His Majesty's Provincial Troops and on actual duty in that service ever since the year one thousand seven hundred and seventy six and remained on such duty until the end of the Rebellion. That your memorialist gave the only intelligence to the *Renown* and two frigates in the North River, of the fire vessels that were fitted out to be sent down upon them so that the men of war were prepared for their reception before they came down, and your memorialist was at his own desire in the *Tryal* Tender ahead of the man of war to receive them. And your memorialist further sheweth that his services were well known to Earl Cornwallis, Lord Chewton and more particularly to Sir William Erskine, Colonel Beverly Robinson, Major Archibald Robinson *[Robertson]* and most of the public officers of the army. Your memorialist also sheweth that Lieutenant Colonel *[Henry]* Bruen who was a Deputy Quarter Master General and was with your memorialist on a Patrol of the Light Dragoons when they stopped at the house where his wife and family resided and a considerable part of your memorialist's effects were lodged just after a party had plundered and taken away every thing. And your memorialist also sheweth that he served the campaign in the Jerseys with Lord Cornwallis in the year one thousand seven hundred and seventy six and commanded the Pioneers in the expedition to Danbury, at the taking of Philadelphia, Charleston, and the relief of Rhode Island.

And your memorialist further sheweth that he is the owner of a house and farm and was in the possession thereof situate in the English Neighborhood in Jersey containing about twenty acres of rich grazing land and worth about seven pound per acre, together with a new brewery not quite finished which the Rebels converted into a store house, and which cost your memorialist with other Improvements ninety pounds <u>Sterling</u>.

And your memorialist further sheweth that he is the owner of a house and farm and was in the possession thereof situate in Bowery Lane, near the City of New York by virtue of a marriage portion containing eight acres of land and would let for thirty pounds Sterling or upwards per annum and is worth at least the sum of seven hundred pounds Sterling.

Your memorialist therefore prays that his case may be taken into your most serious consideration in order that your memorialist may be enabled under your report to receive such aid and relief as his losses may be found to deserve and as a confirmation of the justness of your memorialist's claim as stated in the above petition he refers to William Bayard Esqr. of No. 5 Edward Street Portman Square, Colonel Beverly Robinson at Mortlake, and to the Reverend Garret Lydecker always to be heard of by applying to Mr. Gillham No. 15 Furnivals Inn.

John Aldington was one of three guides who led five thousand Crown forces up the Palisades early in the morning of November 20, 1776. These reenactors portray soldiers of the British Twenty-second Regiment of Foot, after successfully ascending the Palisades for an event in 2007. *Courtesy of David Mutter.*

And to which he later added:

Major Aldington begs leave to state to the Honorable Board of Commissioners that he has charged in his petition which they have been pleased to consider the 22nd Instant, only the sum it first cost him with the charges he has been at in improving it; that the land itself being every foot of it exceeding rich and fertile, with the orchard he had planted and dwelling house, must be worth and would have sold for £20 Currency an acre exclusive of the brewery; that the brewery from its situation being the only establishment of that kind thereabouts; from its proximity to Hackensack and having a water carriage to New York and in the center of a rich populous part of the country, must have turned out to very great advantage. He esteemed it to be the most just and open method of giving in the first cost of his land, building and improvements, that from the opinion the Honorable Board might have of the testimony of his witnesses etc. they might be pleased to fix an estimate. His personal property was considerable, the loss of which he always looked upon as a common consequence attending the rout of an army either friends or foes, therefore never expected nor solicited a compensation. He hopes there is no impropriety in making this statement to the Honorable Commissioners, and prays they will be pleased to take it into consideration.

CHAPTER 2

WEART BANTA

Hackensack

*T*he Banta family, like most in Bergen County, contributed men to both sides of the conflict. Indeed, in addition to this officer, another Weart Banta served in Abraham Van Buskirk's New Jersey Volunteers while a third of the same name served in the Bergen County Militia, fighting against the previous two. The object of this memorial to the Commissioners for Loyalist Claims served the British more as an individual than as part of an organized corps. In November 1778, Banta teamed up with the Continental army deserter turned commander of Refugees Thomas Ward to successfully sneak up to Kakiat with a total of seven volunteers, disarm a guard of eleven Continentals and surprise in their beds the muster master general of the Continental army and his deputy. Then, as James Rivington put it: "the captors brought them to town after many hairbreadth escapes, having by invincible perseverance, surmounted amazing difficulties." One British officer, William Lord Cathcart, told the men, "There had been nothing equal to it since the war began." The capture of these officers followed Banta's previous special service, namely, acting as a guide to Major General Charles Grey in his surprise assault on Colonel George Baylor's Third Light Dragoons in modern River Vale.

For these deeds, Banta was commissioned a lieutenant in the King's Militia Volunteers. This corps was the brainchild of Governor William Franklin, recently exchanged from over two years captivity in Connecticut. Franklin wished to organize those Loyalists who were looking for active service against their countrymen without the constraints, low pay and mundane duties associated with the army. He had barely served two months when a skirmish in Closter put an end to his military career, as the New Jersey Gazette delighted in telling: "put to flight by nine of the militia, commanded by Lieut. J. Huyler, leaving their plunder behind them, and one of their officers, the noted Peter Myer, Ensign in Capt.

Thousands of Loyalists founded Shelburne, Nova Scotia, starting in 1783, briefly making it one of the largest cities in North America at that time. Shown here are some Loyalist-era houses in the historic district of Shelburne. *Courtesy of Todd W. Braisted.*

David Peek's company, dead on the field. Another of their officers was wounded in the arm, and the infamous Weart Banta, so notoriously known for his complicated villainies, thefts, and robberies, was shot through the knee, and it is supposed will, by the amputation of a limb, be disabled from kidnapping and plundering the loyal subjects of this state in future." *While he had no compensation for any property losses, he did receive an annual military allowance of £70 per annum for the remainder of his life, in recognition of his service and disability. Unlike a John Aldington, a Provincial officer who was entitled to half-pay for life in recognition of his service, refugee officers such as Banta had to hope for military allowances or other such rewards for their more irregular services. Banta was commissioned an ensign of the First Company of Refugees embarking for Shelburne, Nova Scotia, in the spring of 1783, starting a new life in what was hoped would be a Loyalist Utopia. After making a living for many years as a carpenter in Shelburne, he removed to Upper Canada, where in 1795 he was petitioning for a new grant of land. His British claim below may be found in AO 13/17/34-35.*

The Memorial of Weart Banta, formerly of Hackensack in the Province of New Jersey but now of Shelburne in Nova Scotia, carpenter, Humbly Sheweth,

That your memorialist was ever most firmly attached to His Majesty's person and government and wholly detested the late unnatural rebellion in America. That he was for many years an inhabitant of Hackensack Town in the County of Bergen and Province of New Jersey.

That in the Year 1774, he being then in New York was obliged to quit the city for being a Tory, or he would have been tarred and feathered for assisting Mr. Alderman Blagg, in taking a Mr. Moore off the cart when the mob were using said Moore very rough. That getting notice that the mob were in pursuit of him, he made his escape to Albany and remained there in peace for some time. That the committees in that city wanting him to sign their association, he was upon his refusal taken up as a Tory, and confined in jail for ten months. That he then made his escape to New York, His Majesty's Forces being in possession thereof where he was employed by Colonel William Bayard and Lieutenant Colonel *[Abraham]* Van Buskirk, to recruit men for their respective regiments, which he did to the number of sixty two recruits (a service at that time performed at the imminent risk of his life) being then assured of a commission in one of their said regiments.

That his knowledge of the country, his activity and zeal in the service of his sovereign acquired him the notice of headquarters, where he was employed in procuring intelligence, acting as a guide, etc. That among many other services, he was sent out on the express purpose of bringing into the lines the infamous *[Abraham]* Brower who had murdered Captain John Richards, which he effected, and afterwards took the Rebel *[Muster Master]* General *[Joseph]* Ward, and *[Lieutenant]* Colonel *[William]* Bradford, with the assistance of only five of his men having first disarmed the general's guard consisting of a sergeant and sixteen men, his errand then being to surprise the post. That he was also sent out by General *[Sir William]* Howe to reconnoiter Fort Montgomery, which he did effectually and afterwards helped to take it. That he was also sent as a guide with the Light Infantry, and fell upon and destroyed Washington's Light Horse. That he was also sent out on expeditions to intercept the Rebel mails. That these services were the sole means of preventing his getting a commission in the new-raised regiments as promised him, he being found much more useful in the scout and reconnoitering duties from his knowledge of the interior country as aforesaid.

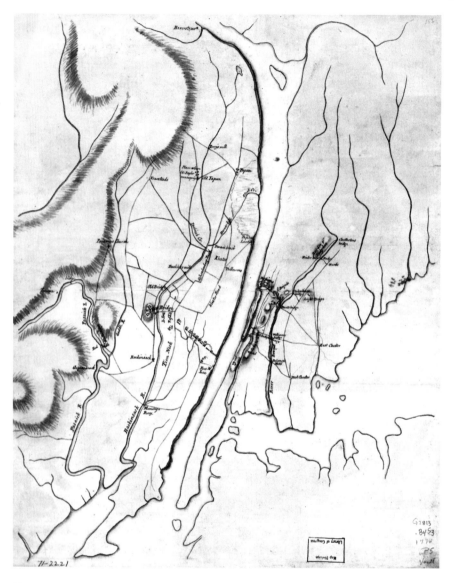

The British were able to carry out their movements in the countryside with relative ease through the use of local guides. Weart Banta led General Grey's column to River Vale where it surprised and defeated Colonel George Baylor's Third Light Dragoons. *Courtesy of the Library of Congress, Washington, D.C.*

That however on the 2nd of February 1779, His Excellency Sir H[enry] Clinton was pleased to give him the commission of lieutenant in the King's Militia Volunteers in which corps he served without pay and that on the 28th day of March following being in a hot engagement with the Rebels he was severely wounded in the knee, which wound has crippled him for the remainder of his days.

That he hath a wife and three small children, living in Shelburne, whom he is unable to maintain, his wound rendering him incapable of those exertions for their support which the rude face of this country absolutely requires, and having by his loyalty and services lost property of various kinds to the amount of between eight and nine hundred pounds New York Currency…

That during the whole of his said services, he was never put upon any pay or regular subsistence, nor hath he received any kind of compensation for such his services and sufferings, either during the war or since…

Your memorialist therefore most humbly prays that his case may be taken into your consideration, in order that he may be enabled, under your report to receive such aid or relief, as his losses and services may be found to deserve. And your memorialist as in duty bound shall pray etc.

CHAPTER 3

HARMAN BLAUVELT

Harrington Township

*H*arman Blauvelt was born May 9, 1761 at Tappan, New York. However, "he removed when quite young to the neighborhood where he now resides on the New Jersey side of the line in Harrington in the county of Bergen where he has resided ever Since," the date of his birth being recorded in the baptism book of the Reformed Dutch Church at Tappan. Harman's service in the Revolution was primarily that of a Bergen County Militiaman but also included a six-month stint in the Continental army as a levy in the Second New Jersey Regiment. Levies were drafts from the militia to fill out the Continental regiments for periods of six to nine months, generally during the time of active campaigning. This enabled the standing army to take the field at nearly full strength during the time of greatest danger. Blauvelt's service in 1780 coincided with Washington's anticipated arrival of ten thousand French troops, who would join in an attack on New York City. With only half the anticipated French expeditionary force arriving at Rhode Island, and those mostly sick, Washington was forced to lay aside his 1780 offensive. His description of Baron de Steuben's commanding in both broken English and French nicely corresponds with popular accounts of the Prussian officer's ignorance of the English language. Serving in 1781 with the militia, Blauvelt took an active part in the actions with Thomas Ward's Loyal Refugee Volunteers at Fort Lee. His U.S. Pension is No. S959.

Harman Blauvelt of the township of Harrington in the county aforesaid being duly Sworn on his oath Saith that he is the same Harman Blauvelt who on the 31st of October 1832 made a declaration and on the 27th of June 1833 answered on oath the interrogatories of the War Department in the Bergen County Inferior Court of Common pleas to obtain a pension under the act of Congress dated June 7th 1832. That he has since making the said declaration and answering the said Interrogatories brought to his recollection some additional facts and circumstances regarding his Services and with more correctness and particularity, than he could in the hurry of business when first called upon state them, and he begs leave to set them forth here by way of Supplement to his declaration. In June 1780 he belonged to Captain Abraham Haring's company of militia at Harrington New Jersey; in that month there was a requisition made by the Legislature of New Jersey on each class of the militia to furnish one recruit for the state regiment in the United States Service, the two classes composing Captain Haring's company determined not to draft by lot from among them but to raise a bounty and hire two recruits for them, and by them with eighty dollars bounty himself and his brother Abraham Blauvelt were hired as the recruits from the company one from each class; they were required to serve until January 1, 1781. From Harrington they went to Preakness accompanied by Major Peter Haring to the house of General *[Colonel]* Dey at Preakness where the army lay and where they were enlisted and given up by General Dey (their Colonel) as part of the quota to be furnished from the militia under his command; here he enlisted in Colonel *[Israel]* Shreve's regiment in the company of Captain Derrick (Richard) Lane, the orderly sergeant was Isaac Willis; this was not long after the battle or skirmish at Springfield as he got the musket of one Harman Pierson who had been wounded at Springfield and was not with the company he recollects this from the fact of Pierson joining the company again when recovered in insisting on the return of his former musket on which he had marked his name. The deponent enlisted in the latter part of June for six months until the 1st of January 1781 according to the requirement of the Legislature. Besides Colonel Shreve, Colonels *[Mathias]* Ogden, *[William]* DeHart and *[Francis]* Barber of the New Jersey line were with the army when he joined them. General *[Anthony]* Wayne with his command lay near them; when they went to Tappan General Washington was with them; he had his headquarters at the house of Frederick Blauvelt, the uncle of deponent in Tappan; while they lay there Major *[John]* André was captured and hung: La Fayette (called by the army Gen. Le Marquis) was with them also at Tappan and was quartered at a farm house near. Baron Steuben was there also instructing the army in tactics and superintending the drills deponent has often been drilled under his direction, he would sit on his horse and give his orders through the officers of the regiment in French or broken English. From Tappan they marched to West Point, the army amounting to about 18,000 men; the deponent there recollects in repairing

Fort Putnam and redoubt No. 4 which *[Benedict]* Arnold had dismounted or dismantled, after leaving West Point they marched to Pompton and went into winter quarters thus, he assisted in building the huts; at the expiration of his time he was solicited to enlist during the war but declined, whereupon the colonel granted discharges to those who had enlisted until the 1st January 1781 in the last day of December when he left the army and came home, and was engaged there at his trade (a weaver) during the winter; shortly after he left the army there was a mutiny in the Jersey line. He knows of none of the company he served with living, except his brother and John Kearn from Morris County, most of them were strangers and enlisted for the war: the names of two of the duty Sergeants were *[James]* Gibson and William Turner; John Ferral, George Griffin, Thomas Hamilton, Harman Pierson, Joseph Babcock and John Paterson were of the company and enlisted for the war. The adjutant of Colonel Shreve's was one *[Luther]* Halsey. John

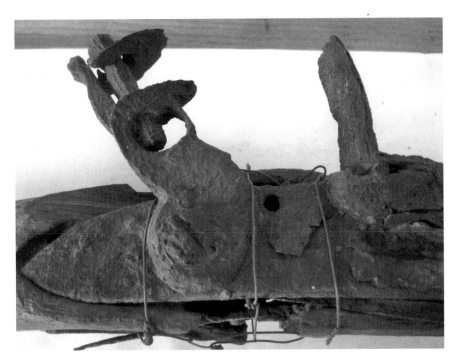

This French Charleville musket, commonly used by Continental troops during the war, undoubtedly has an interesting story to tell. It was fished out of the Hackensack River at New Bridge shortly after the turn of the twentieth century. *Courtesy of the Bergen County Historical Society.*

F. Haring and Garret F. Haring & Cornelius Quackenbush his neighbors belonged to Captain Haring's company at the time deponent was hired by them as their recruit, and the two former have seen deponent in the army while it lay at Tappan.

In the New Jersey militia he served 4 months at separate times in the year 1781, one month he served in April 1781, at Closter under Captain Haring, he was called out by the state authorities under a regulation by which the militia were divided into classes and any number not exceeding one half could be called out for a month. He served out his full month was discharged and returned home; in June 1781, he was again called out on this duty under Captain [Thomas] Blanch served out his month, was discharged and returned home. In the month of August under Captain [John] Huyler and in the month of October under Captain [Elias] Romaine he performed service for one month at each time under the same regulation in each case he

During the time of Blauvelt's six-month service in the Second New Jersey Regiment, Brigadier General Enoch Poor died in camp after a brief illness. He was buried here in September 1780 in the cemetery of the Hackensack Church, where he remains today. *Courtesy of Todd W. Braisted.*

was regularly called out served his month until discharged and then returned home—in all these Services his company was stationed at Closter along the mountain; during the month of April 1781, while in his months service they went with Colonel Dey and the rest of his regiment to drive from Fort Lee (then evacuated and not regularly occupied) a nest of Tories refugees and British who here landed there for the purpose of marauding, But under the cover of a Sloop of war in the stream they disappeared before the militia could get within musket shot of them. This was in April *[May]* 1781 whilst he lay out under Captain Haring.

CHAPTER 4

DAVID RITZEMA BOGERT

Hackensack

*O*ne of the younger residents of the county to take part in the war was David R. Bogert of Hackensack. Although not legally liable for militia service until the age of sixteen, Bogert volunteered two years prior to that, taking part in such actions as the 1777 and 1778 British forages through the county, which, in his claim, he more or less combines into one event. Shortly after turning sixteen, Bogert was taken prisoner, the circumstances of which were duly reported in the July 24, 1779 edition of James Rivington's Royal Gazette: "Early yesterday morning a party of the 4th battalion New-Jersey Volunteers were ordered out by their Lieut. Col. Buskirk under Capt. Van Allen to intercept a gang of rebels, who paint themselves black and commit murders and thefts in Bergen County. Three of them were met at a small distance from the town of Bergen carrying off an inhabitant, but being briskly pushed, two of them were made prisoners, one named David Ritzema Bogert, the other the noted John Loshier [Lozier], who was concerned in the murder of honest Capt. John Richards, and whose repeated instances of villainy had rendered him among the rebels deserving their earliest attention for exchange, when lately taken by a party of the same battalion, who have a second time spared his life." The incident alluded to was the 1778 murder of a Bergen County Loyalist resident, John Richards, by John Lozier and Abraham Brower, two Bergen County militiamen as mentioned in the section on Weart Banta. Bogert spent roughly five months in New York City's Sugar House, which was a warehouse used to lodge land prisoners by the British.

Bogert also relates the incident of the execution of two Loyalists at Hackensack, the only known incident of that sort during the war. This took place on April 9, 1779, as described by the New Jersey Gazette of April 28: "At a Court of Oyer and Terminer held in Bergen County on the 12th ultimo William Cole and

Thomas Welcher alias Straw, were convicted of felony, and executed on Friday the ninth instant. These are worthies by Mr. Robertson, of New-York, in his Royal American Gazette *of the 15th instant, called loyalists. They were famous all over the country for robbery, house-breaking, pocket-picking and horse-stealing, few so eminent in that vocation. Americans may perhaps wonder, but they will be pleased to know these are recommending qualifications in a loyalist." Bogert's application is U.S. Pension No. W3502.*

David R. Bogert being duly sworn doth depose & say that he was born in the City of New York on the 3rd of February 1763 as will appear by his Family record kept by his father until near his decease in 1814, a Record of which may also be found in the Books of the Reformed Dutch Church in New York. That he is now a resident of the town of Malta in Saratoga County New York & in the 70th Year of his age, doth on his oath make the following declaration. That General Washing*[ton]* having retreated through New Jersey was followed by the British Army, Hessians etc. in 1776. There was a considerable number of the People of New Jersey took part with the British, many took protections & others were formed into Regiments and companies, a considerable number of the people of Hackensack where the deponent then resided were so formed under the command of *[Lieutenant]* Colonel *[Abraham Van]* Buskirk. When the Hessians were taken at <u>Trenton</u>, a Spirit of resistance seemed to revive amongst the people, a Company was formed at Hackensack out of the inhabitants who remained true to Whig principles, & engaged to serve as long as their services were required & most of those who escaped the various casualties of a soldier's life did continue to serve till the end of the war in 1783. Whether there was a regular enlistment deponent does not know, but thinks the company chose the officers. John Outwater was Captain, Adam Boyd Lieutenant, Abraham Allen Ensign. Deponent then (the commencement of 1777 & in the 15th Year of his age) joined that company & served with it at Hackensack & vicinity as a volunteer not being then subject to do military duty by Law. The Company were employed in guarding Hackensack, the little-ferry, Polifly, Moonachie, etc. and in scouting parties between the Hackensack & Hudson rivers, the English Neighborhood, Liberty Pole, Fort Lee to Bergen & near Paulus Hook, where the English maintained a garrison during the whole war (except a few hours in 1779 August 16th *[19th]* when our army took it.)

In the Year 1779 the early part of the year neither day nor month recalled the company again engaged to serve the country but whether they were considered as Continental or State Troops deponent does not know.

REGULATIONS UNDER THE ACT OF JUNE 7, 1832.

The following regulations have been adopted:

This law has been construed to extend, as well to the line, as to every branch of the Staff of the Army, and to include under the terms "Continental Line," "State troops," "militia," and "volunteers," all persons enlisted, drafted, or who volunteered and who were bound to military service, but not those who were occasionally employed with the army upon civil contracts, such as Clerks to Commissaries and to Store Keepers, &c. Teamsters, Boatmen, &c. Persons who served on board of Private Armed Vessels are also excluded from the benefits of the law, as well as persons who turned out as patrols, or were engaged in guarding particular places at night, and were not recognized as being in actual military service.

Four general classes of cases are embraced in this law:
1. The Regular Troops.
2. The State Troops, Militia, and Volunteers.
3. Persons employed in the Naval service.
4. Indian Spies.

As rolls of the regular troops in the Revolutionary War exist in this Department, all persons, claiming the benefit of this law as officers, non-commissioned officers, musicians or privates, will in the first instance, make application by transmitting the following declaration, which will be made before a Court of Record of the County where such applicant resides. And every Court having by law a seal and Clerk is considered a Court of Record.

DECLARATION,

In order to obtain the benefit of the Act of Congress of the 7th of June, 1832.

State, Territory, or District of ⎰
County of ⎱ *ss.*

On this   day of   personally appeared (a) before

A. B. a resident (b) of   in the county of   and State, Territory or District of   aged (c)   years, who being first duly sworn, according to law, doth on his oath make the following declaration, in order to obtain the benefit of the provion made by the act of Congress, passed June 7th, 1832. That he enlisted in the Army of the United States in the year (d)   , with   and served in the   (e) regiment of the   line, under the following named officers:

[Here set forth the names and rank of the Field and Company Officers; the time he left the service; (and if he served under more than one term of enlistment, he must specify the particular period, and rank and names of his officers;) the town or county and State in which he resided when he enered the service; the battles, if any, in which he was engaged, and the country through which he marched.   ☞ This form is to be varied so as to apply to the cases of officers and persons who belonged to the militia, volunters, navy, &c.]

He hereby relinquishes every claim (f) whatever to a pension or an annuity, except the present, and he declares that his name is not on the Pension Roll of any Agency in any State, or (if any) only on that of the Agency in the State of

Sworn to and subscribed the day and year aforesaid.   A. B.

An extract of the U.S. pension act allowing veterans of the Revolution to receive aid in their old age. *Courtesy of the National Archives and Records Administration, Washington, D.C.*

The company then chose Abraham Huysman for ensign and the Captain (Outwater) appointed deponent a corporal and the following day deponent acted as corporal & continued so to act till he was taken prisoner in a skirmish at Bergen, & after his exchange in December returning his duties in the company he continued so to act till some time in February following.

And this deponent remarks that Captain Outwater's Company were completely isolated and acted during these three Years independently of all other troops as he thinks and believes. Lord Cornwallis came up with 5,000 men & lay in the vicinity several weeks. Still this company though actively engaged in various military duties were not in company with Continental troops & when in 1778 Lord Cornwallis with 7,000 men came through Hackensack & went five miles South West to the Passaic River & then returned and lay three weeks at the New Bridge, although the Regiment of Militia composing all the militia of Bergen County under Colonel Theunis Dey were called out and Colonel *[William]* Malcom with the 5th New York Regiment came to Paramus, & Colonel *[George]* Baylor's Regiment of light dragoons had lain there part of the summer & although Major *[blank]* (name forgot) with some men from Somerset were sent to Hackensack & Brigadier General *[Nathaniel]* Heard with some militia and an old iron 9 pounder came into the place in pursuit of part of Cornwallis's army, still our orders were received from Captain *[John]* Outwater. In 1779 Captain *[Thomas]* Blanch commanded a company, Captain *[Elias]* Romaine another, Captain *[John]* Hopper another, north of Hackensack extending their services to Tappan, Nyack & other places north & to Paulus Hook South and some time to Hackensack; also Colonel *[Christian]* Febiger with the *[2nd]* Regiment *[of]* Virginians laid there also, & the North Carolina line at Paramus 9 miles west. These last kept a guard at the little ferry, which was taken by the English troops & deponent found Sergeant Smith and some others he knew prisoners in the Sugar House in 1779.

The Deponent further declares that during those three years he does not know that Captain Outwater received any orders from any of the Continental officers which laid at Hackensack or the vicinity or from Colonel *[Theunis]* Dey who commanded the Militia Regiment of Bergen County, but that on one Occasion of Executing two felons the Sheriff Boyd called out the Posse Comitatus being apprehensive of a rescue by the British parties in the vicinity. Our company formed part of it & had previously guarded the goal. On another occasion the major of Colonel Baylor's Regiment named *[Alexander]* Clough commanded in the absence of Colonel Baylor. The quarter master of the regiment pressed a quantity of grain at the house of a farmer named Berry for the use of the regiment & Berry took out a writ for the quarter master & Clough refused leave to the sheriff to execute the writ, the sheriff called out the Posse when the regiment of militia assembled and our company were also assembled to assist the sheriff. But good men in the place interfered & the major allowed the writ to be served. The major was soon after killed when the Regiment was massacred at *[Old]* Tappan.

The deponent further declares that in 1779, he drew rations of flour, pork & whiskey till he was taken prisoner and on eight dollars as one month's pay & that was all the compensation he ever received, except that the State of New Jersey has since the war paid him for his musket & accoutrements taken with him.

Deponent resided a few months during 1780 at Kinderhook & then at Preakness near the head quarters of General Washington where he joined the militia company of Captain *[John]* Mead, Colonel Dey's regiment and with them went on the lines *[in]* 1781 where Captain *[Thomas]* Ward was building a second blockhouse on the spot that General *[Anthony]* Wayne had unsuccessfully attempted to take in 1780, and after some fighting drove him on board his galleys in the North River and demolished the blockhouse. While on the lines deponent was detached with a party & served under Captain *[John]* Hopper. During the last year of the war the deponent returned to Hackensack & under the command of Captain Outwater but cannot say how long he served, & that he has resided in New York *[City]*, Dutchess County New York & Malta since the war. Deponent further says that after the law had passed under which he claims a pension he went to Hackensack & after much enquiry found that Captain Outwater was dead & had left no papers. Ensign Huysman is dead. Lieutenant Boyd being sheriff never had any of the company papers & of all the men with whom he served and retain their memory of his services Silvester Maurice *[Marius]* and Henry Berdan are all that are left and only three others are living two of whom are entirely childith and Lieutenant Boyd now 86 years old & very sick emphatically said "My dear sir, you and your family have suffered every thing & if any thing can be got, you ought to have it, but how can you expect that I, 86 years old & nearly in the grave should remember Your services?"

Deponent further says these services were rendered fifty three years since, meaning the most recent of them, and his own memory being impaired by a long severe fit of sickness as well as by time and the usual occurrences which take place in fifty five years of a mans life, he has not been able to remember many of the events of his military life but that there was little rest for the soldiers of that period. Deponent further says that he has recently been informed that Ensign John Terhune who commanded the party when deponent was taken is living near Detroit & detailed to his informant the circumstance of deponents being taken & his *[illegible]*. Deponent further says that when taken by Buskirk's Regiment he was carried into New York before Major General James Patterson *[Pattison]* then British Commandant in New York & in the street he was separated from his companion John Lozier (who was taken with him) he was sent to the Provost kept by *[William]* Cunningham & deponent to the Sugar House kept by Sergeant Hulton & that he has not been able to find a man living of 300 who were confined there at that time.

And further the deponent says that the company held their head quarters in Hackensack & never were encamped nor were the Militia Regiment or even the Continental Light Horse or Foot regiments or parties—it was not the fashion in those days. They laid in houses & barns in woods & swamps

Captain John Outwater was an active commander of militia and state troops during the war. His remains are buried at the small Outwater Cemetery in Carlstadt, in the southern part of the county. *Courtesy of Todd W. Braisted.*

Before he was vice president of the United States, courted Theodosia Bartow Prevost at the Hermitage or shot and killed Alexander Hamilton in a duel in Weehawken, a young Aaron Burr served as a Continental army officer, killing and capturing several men from a British picket guard near New Bridge in September 1777. *Courtesy of the Library of Congress, Washington, D.C.*

& open fields on the ground. The company generally maintained a guard at the little ferry & in the town & generally a party were scouting towards Paulus Hook. Parties of the enemy often came up from Paulus Hook & sometimes other places & plundered the place. One party burnt the house of the sheriff and the court house. Another came to Moonachie and killed three of our citizens & wounded three others & were repulsed by a part of our Company in which I was. Another party came to the same place & were again repulsed by our Company I was there then 18 of the company with Lieutenant Boyd, were sent to surprise the British picket of Lord Cornwallis *[Sir Henry Clinton]* in 1778 *[1777]*, & when we came into the guard house (Timpany's School house) we found it empty. Colonel *[Aaron]* Burr had taken the picket without firing & carried them away and the enemy seemed then not to know their picket was taken. It is impossible for deponent at this distance of time to remember the various skirmishes in which he was engaged with parts of his own & other companies: Silvester Maurice, Henry Denny, James Chappel, Abraham Allen, Peter Allen, Morris Earl & others were wounded and others were wounded also but their names forgot.

If it is required that deponent should name Officers whom he knew it would make a long list—Lieutenants Wrisenfels, Bagley, & Frelich were schoolmates—he knew most of the officers of the New York line—Some of the Virginia line—Colonel *[Moses]* Hazen & some of his officers—Colonel *[John]* Lamb & many of his—Colonel *[Thomas]* Procter & many of his regiment—Colonel Baylor, Major *[Henry]* Lee & his—Captain Van Livearingen, Colonel *[Frederick]* Wisenfelt, Colonel *[Marinus]* Willett etc. etc.

Deponent further says that as his engagements were not for any particular period as far as he now remembers so when on very short notice he was going to Kinderhook & apprized his captain of it, the captain did not offer him a discharge, nor did deponent ask for one or think one necessary.

The Deponent further states that he has now brought forward the evidence of Silvester Maurice & Henry Berdan in confirmation of his own statement both of whom he knew & was known by them thro' the whole war & that he is known by many of the inhabitants of Ballston & Malta in Saratoga County. Deponent further declares that he has not heretofore made any application for a pension under any former law of Congress. And that Elder M Swain, Henry Doolittle *[and]* Moses Williams are well acquainted with deponent's character for veracity & their belief of his services as a soldier of the Revolution.

And deponent further states that he served under Captain Outwater at least three years in these Years 1777, 1778 & 1779 including the time he was a prisoner of war.

And this deponent hereby relinquishes every claim whatever to a pension or annuity except the present and declares that his name is not on the pension roll of the agency of this or any other state.

CHAPTER 5

JANE, DAVID AND GILLIAM DEMAREST

Hackensack Township

*T*here is no better example of the effects of war on a single family than that of the family of David G. and Jane Demarest of Hackensack Township. It is not unusual today for a husband and wife to differ in their political views. But in times of war, most couples tend to stay united in a common cause. In the course of a civil war however, which the Revolution in Bergen County most certainly was, opposing views may become exasperated, tearing a family asunder. Such was the case of the Demarest family.

David G. Demarest certainly manifested a loyalty to the King early on, enlisting on November 23, 1776, in Captain William Van Allen's Company of the Fourth Battalion, New Jersey Volunteers. His service was but two weeks, being taken prisoner on December 6 of that year, possibly during the unit's raid on Tappan of that date. Trying to piece together his whereabouts after that, with the documents available, seems to indicate he was released and went home, but exactly when is unclear. On May 16, 1779, a body of about one thousand British troops, including the Fourth Battalion, New Jersey Volunteers, entered Bergen County and drove away the picket at New Bridge. It was also on this day that David Demarest is listed as having rejoined the battalion. It seems likely Demarest was at home nearby and took the opportunity of joining his old unit. For the next few months, however, he does not appear present with them on the rolls, listed recruiting at Kingsbridge in September and detained by New York's town major in October. By December, he disappears altogether from the rolls. At this time, Demarest appears to have been discharged from the New Jersey Volunteers and became one of the original members of Thomas Ward's Loyal Refugee Volunteers, which was formed in November 1779. He is definitely listed as one of the 110 defenders of the

Bull's Ferry Blockhouse when attacked by Anthony Wayne's troops that following July and still listed on their rolls in 1782, as David Demerea, a name also used by the family. His indictment for high treason in Bergen County was published in the New Jersey Gazette *on November 22, 1780. Ward and his men abandoned their final post at Bergen Point in October 1782 and became the first Loyalists to set sail for a new life in Nova Scotia. Demarest would accompany them, eventually ending up as a resident in Upper Canada. But he would make that journey alone. Demarest's brief claim for compensation for his losses, located in TNA's AO 13/81/73, appears as follows:*

A true and just account of losses sustained, by David Demare, late an inhabitant in the County of Bergen, and Province of New Jersey, on account of his loyalty and attachment to the British Government, viz.

	£	S	D
150 Acres of land, on which stood a stone house containing 3 rooms, 1 frame barn 45 feet by 50, for which he was offered in the year 1773 £ 2800, which he now values at	2000.	0.	0.
1 Horse	15	0.	0.
3 Milk cows & 1 calf	16.	0.	0.
18 Sheep 10/.	9.	0.	0.
1 Iron bound wagon & utensils	10.	0.	0.
Farming utensils	3.	0.	0.
New York Currency £	2053.	0.	0.

The above David Demare joined His Majesty's Army on their arrival in New York, and entered as a soldier in the 2nd *[4th]* Battalion, New Jersey Volunteers, in which station he served for the term of three years, during which time and after he served (at different times) as guides to the royal army.

A sergeant and private of the re-created Fourth Battalion, New Jersey Volunteers chat during a public program at Historic New Bridge Landing. *Courtesy of Todd W. Braisted.*

15 April 1786

It is interesting to note he makes no mention of his capture or later service with the Refugees. David made his new life in Canada alone as he had left behind his wife, Jane, and their children. It was not that Jane lacked an opportunity to join her husband; as a good Whig, she simply had no inclination to do so. While standing up for her principles was one thing, the law was another. When her husband left home in May 1779 to once again join the British, the state went to work confiscating the estate, which unfortunately for Jane and her family, was in David's name. She quickly petitioned Governor William Livingston and the legislature to have the property transferred to the rest of the family in an effort to stave off confiscation. Below is her 1779 petition, preserved today in the New Jersey State Archives:

The Petition of Jane Demarest of the Precinct of Hackensack in the County of Bergen In behalf of herself and her distressed children humbly sheweth

That whereas David G. Demarest of the Precinct of Hackensack and County of Bergen hath in May last deserted his country and family and joined the troops of the King of Great Britain, and thereby exposed your petitioner and her children to poverty and want, and the penalty of a law which though just, yet in this instance seems rather severe.

That your petitioner has incurred the reproaches and hatred of her husband and many of her family connections by means of her attachment to the interests of America and her zeal in instilling those principles in her Children.

That your petitioner's oldest son, the only one capable of bearing arms, notwithstanding his Father's commands to the contrary, when the enemy were already in possession of the New Bridge, swam across Hackensack River and joined the militia of this county under the command of Colonel *[Theunis]* Dey, and has since engaged in the regiment formed for the defense of the frontiers of this state.

Your petitioner farther appeals to all those acquainted with her conduct and character for the truth of those facts specified as above, and for her uniform and inflexible attachment to the just cause of America and therefore prays that the title of the estate formerly belonging to David G. Demarest aforesaid now vested in the state, may by an act of this state be transferred to your petitioner and to the heirs forever.

Your petitioner casts herself and her helpless family under the protection of her countrymen hoping to receive at their hands that clemency and tenderness, which has been denied her by a cruel and unnatural husband, trusting in the wisdom and tenderness of the representation of a free people, she as in duty bound shall ever pray etc.

Subjoined to Jane's petition was the following certificate of support, signed by many of the county's leading Whigs.

We the underwritten being well acquainted with the steady attachment of the subscriber of the within petition & fully convinced of the equity and justice of the prayer of the said petition, do with the greatest *[illegible]* join in the prayer of the aforesaid petitioner and hereunto affixed our hands, not doubting but that the petitioner will find that protection to keep aforesaid property is the wish of the Honorable Legislature, that her cruel said husband For *[illegible]* her.

County of Bergen
September 13th 1779

[signed]

David Demarest Lieutenant	Peter R. Fell
Abraham Brewer	Jacob Terhune Justice of the Peace
Elias Romaine Captain	Isaac Vanderbeck Justice of the Peace
Jacob Campbell	James Board
Isack Romyn	Hendricus Kuyper } Commissioners
William Campbell	Garret Lydecker
Daniel Vorhis	
John Mauritius Goetschius Major	
John Cooper	
Samuel Bradhurst	
Samuel Demarest Captain	
Harmanus Van Huysen Lieutenant	
Huryem *[?]*	

[docketed]

Petition from Jane Demarest setting forth that her husband is gone to the enemy, & praying that his estate may descend to his children in consideration of their services. Read September 27, 1779. Ordered to be referred to the next assembly.

The eldest son that Jane Demarest mentioned was Gilliam. Gilliam Demarest had passed away in 1811, but his widow, Bridget, applied for a pension under a later act providing for wives of deceased veterans. Benjamin Romaine, a fellow veteran, testified on behalf of Bridget:

> That the said Gilliam Demarest's father David Demarest deserted his country's cause, and eloped to the enemy services to the City of New York, and continued there during the war, and his farm was confiscated...The said father repeatedly requested, and demanded his said son Gilliam to join him in New York, but the son held to his integrity to the end of the war. That he was taken a prisoner, and exchanged, nevertheless his father's commands, and again went into military service—was severely wounded in individual contest in the hand in a personal contest with an enemy Refugee, who sought to capture him, as I have full and satisfactory information of this fact.

Philip Demarest, in 1841, likewise testified:

...in the year 1781, this deponent & the aforesaid Gilliam Demarest was again called out in the service under Captain Samuel Demarest and that on or about the [July 27] in the year aforesaid this deponent & the aforesaid Gilliam Demarest at the Hackensack New Bridge, while on duty was surprised and taken prisoners of war by the enemy and taken from thence to the City of New York and confined in the Sugar House & this deponent remained there six months & was then exchanged and this deponent further says when he left for home the aforesaid Gilliam Demarest yet remained there as a prisoner of war.

Not only was Gilliam Demarest, along with John and Philip Demarest, taken prisoner that July day in 1781, but they were taken prisoner by the Loyal Refugee Volunteers, David G. Demarest's unit. The Royal Gazette *for August 1, 1781, carried news of the capture: "On Sunday evening last a party of Loyal Refugees under the command of Major Thomas Ward, went out from Bergen Neck, as far as the Liberty Pole. Major Ward detached Captain John Miller with a party of twenty horse, who penetrated as far as the New Bridge, near Hackensack, and captured three notorious rebels by the names of Demareas, drove off their stock, and returned to the party without firing a shot." Thomas Ward, in his official report to Major Oliver DeLancey, Jr. wrote on July 31:*

Surgeons on each side looked after the health and welfare of the troops under their care. This receipt shows a common procedure administered for a stomach ailment, given to a soldier in Captain Outwater's State Troops in 1781. *Courtesy of the National Archives and Records Administration, Washington, D.C.*

I immediately on receipt of your letter on Sunday last set off to Bergen, and sent two men into the country towards King's Ferry and directly proceeded after them myself, with a party of about one hundred and fifty horse and foot with a brass field piece as far as the Liberty Pole. I then Detached Captain Miller with twenty horsemen to the house of Captain [Samuel] Demarea, but he had taken Flight. He captured three notorious Rebels and afterwards joined the foot without a shot fired at him or the party.

The American Revolution left this family imprisoned, exiled and homeless, despite fighting for both the winners and losers.

CHAPTER 6

SAMUEL DEMAREST

New Bridge

*S*amuel Demarest began as a private in 1776 but quickly advanced to the rank of *captain in the Bergen County Militia less than three years later. A resident of New Bridge, Demarest did both militia duty and raised companies to serve as state troops, particularly a company of twelve months men, embodied militia serving for a fixed period of time. Benjamin Romaine, one of his soldiers, said of him: "The services of Captain Demarest, both from precept and example, were highly serviceable to our country's cause." A return of troops at Fort Lee on September 29, 1776, shows 131 officers and men of the Bergen County Militia stationed there, most likely working on the construction of the works and serving as wagoners like Samuel Demarest. The fort served in conjunction with Fort Washington on the opposite side of the Hudson, in an attempt to close the river to British shipping. The heavy guns mounted high on the cliffs of the Palisades were generally safe from return fire from the British, although the work could prove extremely dangerous, as related by General Henry Knox of the Continental Artillery to his wife Lucy, speaking of one of his officers: "Young [Captain] Hardy Peirce had his head shot off by an accident when firing at the enemy's ships on 5th November." In 1781, Demarest was in command of a company of State Troops. State Troops were essentially militia called into service for three, six, nine or twelve consecutive months' service. There were several companies of these troops serving in the county, and elsewhere in the state, throughout the war. These orders, issued in Trenton on December 26, 1780, show the formation of Captain Outwater's Company. Those issued for Captain Demarest would have been very similar:*

Officers such as Samuel Demarest enjoyed more creature comforts than the average soldier. This reconstructed hut at Fort Lee Historic Park would be a comfortable home for two lower-ranking officers. *Courtesy of Todd W. Braisted.*

Be it therefore enacted by the Council and General Assembly of this State, and it is hereby enacted by the authority of the Same that eight hundred and twenty men shall be raised by voluntary enlistment and embodied for the defense of the frontiers of this state, to continue in service until the first day of January one thousand seven hundred and eighty two unless sooner discharged and to be stationed in the several counties in such a manner as to afford the most equal and beneficial protection to all the inhabitants on the said frontiers, and that the said eight hundred and twenty men be distributed and stationed in the different counties as follows that is to say, in the County of Bergen, one hundred and twenty men to be divided into two companies, consisting of sixty men each including three commissioned officers, three sergeants, three corporals, one drummer, and three horsemen: one to be raised and commanded by Captain John Outwater of the County of Bergen...

Demarest's pension application is registered as No. S15081.

On this Fourth day of September 1832, personally appeared in open court before the judges of the Court of Common Pleas in and for the County of Saratoga *[New York]* now sitting, Samuel Demarest a resident of the town of Waterford in the County of Saratoga aforesaid, aged eighty seven years who being first duly sworn according to law doth on his oath make the following declaration in order to obtain the benefit of the Act of Congress passed June 7, 1832.

That he entered the service of the United States under the following named officers & served as herein stated viz. in the latter part of the summer of the year 1776 & before the British landed or came into *[Sandy]* Hook at New York; the militia of that part of New Jersey where deponent resided were ordered out to Elizabethtown (N.J.) That deponent on that occasion turned out as a soldier and went to Elizabethtown. That he marched through the Village of Hackensack, Acquackanonk, Second River and Newark to Elizabethtown aforesaid. That they remained there a few days *[and]* were then ordered to Fort Bergen opposite N.Y. remained there a few days and were then ordered to Fort Lee when the troops built a fort and remained some short time and were then discharged. That deponent at this time was out in actual service about one month and the names of his officers as far as he can now recollect them were Captain Cooper, Colonel Theunis Dey & General *[William]* Winds. That there were no regular officers at the above named posts at the time deponent was there, according to his best recollection. That Washington's army at the time lay on Long Island. That the British landed at the time deponent was stationed at Elizabethtown aforesaid.

And this deponent further saith that shortly after he returned home from the aforesaid month's service he was pressed with his wagon and horses into the service and taken to Fort Lee & from thence to Fort Washington on York Island & from thence he removed a load of sick and retreated up to White Plains about the time that Fort Washington was taken. That he was at White Plains at the time of the battle in the capacity of a teamster as aforesaid. That the next day after the battle he was discharged and returned home. That in the latter part of the year 1776 deponent received a sergeant's warrant in Captain Lozier's Company & Colonel Theunis Dey's Regiment of the New Jersey Militia which situation he held till the year 1779, when he received a captain's commission which he retained till the close of the war.

Over one hundred Bergen County militia, including Samuel Demarest, helped garrison Fort Lee in the early autumn of 1776. The fort's primary purpose was to deny free passage of the Hudson for the British Royal Navy, utilizing heavy artillery firing thirty-two-pound shot, such as the gun pictured here. *Courtesy of Todd W. Braisted.*

That deponent at the commencement of the war resided at New Bridge (N.J.) within about fourteen miles of New York and six of Fort Lee. That the inhabitants of that part of the country were greatly exposed to and suffered much from the foraging, marauding and other parties of the enemy who were making repeated and continued incursions into the country from New York & Fort Lee. That that district of country was through the whole war on account of its vicinity to the enemy in an almost constant and continued state of alarm; in consequence whereof the militia of the neighborhood were so repeatedly called out to protect the country as to make their service amount almost to a continued and a constant service. That during the time deponent held his sergeant's warrant and lieutenant's commission aforesaid, he verily believes he was engaged in actual military service one half of the whole time. The precise times when called out and the length of the periods at the several times that he served he can not state. That almost every day or every few days he was called out, would remain under arms until the hostile parties retreated or were repelled and then return home. That he has no doubt that he was out upon military service during the time he was lieutenant as aforesaid more than one year in the whole made up of short periods of service of the kind above mentioned and when not actually under arms he was unable to attend to his business or even to remain at home except by stealth on account of his exposure to capture from the enemy in consequence of his being an officer and obnoxious to the enemy they having made repeated attempts to effect his capture from his own home.

And the deponent further saith that on or about the 23rd day of January 1779 he received a commission from Governor Livingston of the State of New Jersey [as] captain in the militia of the last mentioned state. That the aforesaid commission bears date on the day & year last aforesaid and is hereto annexed. That shortly after he received the aforesaid captain's commission deponent was directed by Governor Livingston aforesaid to raise a company of men, by enlistment for one year for the purpose mainly of guarding the lines. That deponent raised the said company accordingly and immediately called them into actual service. That deponent with his company were stationed for the year at New Bridge. That he was in the regiment commanded by Colonel Dey and in the brigade of General Winds. That deponent's lieutenant was David Demarest & his Ensign [blank] Brackett. That there were no regular troops stationed there at the time. That from the time deponent raised the aforesaid company in the year 1779 he was in the military service as captain about four years. That he was not engaged in any general battle but in a great number of skirmishes with parties of the enemy.

To the first interrogatory proposed in the instructions of the Secretary at War, and now propounded to the witness by the court here in session the deponent says that he was born in Hackensack, Bergen Co. N.J. on the 15th August 1745.

To the second interrogatory the deponent saith that he hath no record of his age. 'Twas recorded in Family Bible & probably in the records of the Dutch Church at Hackensack; deponent does not know where the Family Bible is or whether in existence.

To the third interrogatory deponent saith that he was living at New Bridge in the Precinct of Hackensack, New Jersey at the time he was called into the service. That he continued his residence there until the year 1792, then moved up into the town of Broadalbin, Montgomery County N.Y. where he resided till in or about the year 1820 when his wife died & he broke up house-keeping, since which time he has staid about at different places with his children & friends, much of the time at Broadalbin aforesaid & the town adjoining, some part of the time at Watervliet in the County of Albany and considerable of the time at Waterford in the county of Saratoga where he now resides.

To the fourth interrogatory the deponent answered that he was called into service by the order of his superior officers. That in the year 1776 while he was a private and a non-commissioned officer he was ordered out in common with the other militia men and after he received his commissions of lieutenant and captain he was ordered out by his superior officers.

To the fifth interrogatory the deponent saith that there were no Regular officers or troops stationed at the places where deponent lay while in the service according to his recollection. That deponent was attached to Colonel Theunis Dey's Regiment and General Wind's Brigade. That he does not recollect the names of any other militia officers or regiments at the places where deponent was stationed then those hereinafter mentioned and as it respects the general circumstances of the deponent's service he refers to his declaration hereinbefore set forth names of militia officers, Major Richard Dey, 2nd Major John Goetschius, two Captain Hoppers, [John] Outwater, [Thomas] Blanch, Hernden, [Joseph] Board & [David] Van Bussen also captains.

To the sixth interrogatory the deponent saith that he did receive a lieutenant's commission as in said declaration is mentioned, does not recollect by whom it was signed nor what has become of it. That he also received a captain's commission as is stated in the foregoing declaration which was signed by Governor Livingston of New Jersey and is hereunto annexed.

To the seventh interrogatory the deponent saith that John B. Steel a clergyman of the Reformed Dutch Church in the town of Watervliet in the County of Albany and Moses Scott Esquire of the town of Waterford in the County of Saratoga well know deponent and have so known him for many years past and will testify as to the good character of deponent for veracity, and to their belief in his services as a soldier of the Revolution.

And this deponent further saith that he hath no documentary evidence of his service except the annexed commission of captain, and he hereby relinquishes every claim whatever to a pension, or annuity except the present and declares that his name is not on the Pension Roll of the agency of any state.

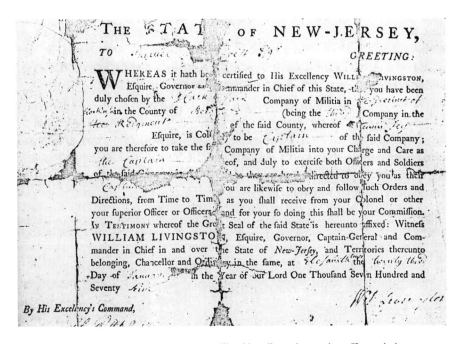

The commission was the legal document utilized by all armies to give officers their authority. Commissions in the militia, such as Captain Demarest's pictured here, were signed by the governor of their state (or province). *Courtesy of the National Archives and Records Administration, Washington, D.C.*

To which was annexed Captain Demarest's commission as captain, here transcribed verbatim:

The STATE of NEW-JERSEY,

To Samuel Demarest Esqr. Greeting:

WHEREAS it hath been certified to His Excellency William Livingston, Esquire, Governor and Commander in Chief of this State, that you have been duly chosen by the Hackensack Company of Militia in the precinct of Hackensack in the County of Bergen (being the third) Company in the Regiment of the said County, whereof Theunis Dey Esquire, is Colonel; to be Captain of the said Company; you are therefore to take the said Company of Militia into your Charge and Care as the Captain thereof, and duly to exercise both Officers and Soldiers of the said Company in Arms. And as they are hereby directed to obey you as their Captain. You are likewise to obey and follow such Orders and Directions, from Time to Time, as you shall receive from your Colonel or other your superior Officer or Officers, and for your so doing this shall be your Commission. In Testimony whereof the Great Seal of the said State is hereunto affixed: Witness WILLIAM LIVINGSTON, Esquire, Governor, Captain-General and Commander in Chief in and over the State of New-Jersey, and Territories thereunto belonging, Chancellor and Ordinary in the same, at Elizabethtown the twenty third Day of January in the Year of our Lord One Thousand Seven Hundred and Seventy Nine.

Wil. Livingston

By His Excellency's Command,
Chas. Pettit Secy.

CHAPTER 7

JOHN DEVOE

Teaneck

*B*orn in Manhattan on February 16, 1763, John Devoe was a resident of Hackensack Township by the time he was old enough for military service, which he did at the age of sixteen. After two years serving in tours of duty in the militia, Devoe entered the state troops under Captain Samuel Demarest on April 1, 1781. State Troops were in effect nothing more than militia embodied for three, six, nine or twelve months of continuous service. Demarest's Company was small—only twelve or thirteen men according to Major Goetschius. Stationed at New Bridge to cover that vital crossing, they likewise patrolled far and wide, guarding against their primary adversary, Major Thomas Ward and his corps of Refugees. On May 14, 1781, Demarest happily reported to the governor: "on the 10th instant I marched out with a detachment of men as far as Wehock [Weehawken] and the next morning I fell in with a party of Refugees driving down some cattle and horses, which I attacked them and retook the cattle and horses and killed two of the enemy and returned without the loss of a man." Their triumph over Ward's men was short-lived, as later that very day, Demarest's men, as well as the county's militia, were engaged by the Refugees, who had landed near Fort Lee to establish a new post on the ruins of the fort. This event, as Devoe details, significantly impacted his state of health. The action is described in detail by the New-York Gazette and the Weekly Mercury:

> Last Monday morning, the 14th instant, a party of about 70 Loyal Refugees, (who had evacuated the post at Bergen-Point) under the command of Captain Ward, being joined by an equal number from this place, under the command of Captain George Harden, landed at Bull's Ferry, on the Jersey shore, from whence they proceeded by the way of Fort

Lee to the English Neighborhood, from which place they returned to Fort Lee at evening of the same day; soon after which a party of about 100 rebels made their appearance and took possession of a stone house at the distance of about an hundred yards from Fort Lee, from whence they kept up a constant fire, for near an hour, when it was determined to dispossess them by storming the house, which they perceiving, very prudently took to their heels, leaving one man killed, and the Refugees made two more prisoners. But they having received a reinforcement of 300 militia, and one years men, made their appearance again, the next morning, in three divisions, meditating an attack, which those brave Loyalists being apprized of, immediately marched out, and commenced the attack, the enemy at the same time faced to the right about, and fled in great confusion, (many of them throwing away their arms) leaving on the field wounded their Colonel Cooper, who is also a Judge and Commissioner for selling the estates of the Loyalists, also two men killed.

After being wounded and taken prisoner, Devoe was soon exchanged and returned to duty but saw no further action in the war. Following the war, Devoe left New Jersey to head north, living in Broadalbin, New York, for about ten years, followed by five years in Johnstown and finally in the town of Homer, New York, where he had resided twenty-six years at the time of his filing a pension request.

On this 29th day of April 1834 personally appeared in open court before the Court of Common Pleas of the County of Cortland now sitting, John Devoe a resident of the town of Homer, County of Cortland & State of New York, aged 71 years who being first duly sworn according to law doth on his own oath make the following declaration in order to obtain the benefit of the Act of Congress passed June 7, 1832 to wit that according to the best of his recollection he enlisted into the United States Service in the Revolutionary war on the 1st of April 1781 for the term of one year in the Company commanded by Captain Samuel Demarest in Colonel *[Theunis]* Dey's Regiment of New Jersey Militia at Hackensack in New Jersey the place where this deponent was brought up from a boy. That on the 14th May 1781 in a skirmish near Fort Lee, this deponent was severely wounded across the head by a blow with a broad sword from a British Dragoon. This deponent was also at the same time wounded by a blow from a musket against his temple, also by a blow from the britch of a gun & stabbed with a bayonet, two of his

Thomas Ward's Loyalist woodcutters built several blockhouses for their defense during the course of their two and a half years in Bergen County, including those at Bull's Ferry and Bergen Point. This reproduction is a recent addition to Fort Lee Historic Park. *Courtesy of Todd W. Braisted.*

ribs were broken, his back injured & slightly grazed with a musket ball. This deponent was left for dead on the field & was taken prisoner, but exchanged in about ten days & so far recovered from his wounds that he joined his company in about seven weeks & served out his year & was discharged at the expiration of his years service by Captain Demarest at New Bridge in Hackensack, but did not receive any written discharge. This deponent in consequence of the said wounds has always been afflicted although he was not so much so for a few years after receiving the wounds as he has been since. He is now nearly deprived of the use of his limbs & wholly unable to labor from the effects of the bayonet wound. In the month of June 1807 he was placed on the Invalid Pension List at $2 per month to commence August 1, 1806 & his pension has since been increased at different times so that he now draws $8 per month at the New York Agency. This deponent served over one year in the army of the Revolution in the New Jersey Militia in

An unknown veteran of the American Revolution, buried at Hackensack Church. Note the marker from the Sons of the American Revolution, indicating his status as a soldier from the war. *Courtesy of Todd W. Braisted.*

Col. Dey's Regiment previous to the years service under Captain Demarest. He commenced serving in the army in the year 1779 & served under the following officers to wit Captains *[Thomas]* Blanch, *[John]* Outwater, *[Elias]* Romaine & *[James]* Christie. His services were usually for one month at a time; this deponent would go & serve one month & then return home & deponent's father would take his place & serve a month. His services in this way commenced early in the year 1779 & continued until he enlisted under Captain Demarest but it is totally impossible for him to specify the date of each service under the said Blanch, Outwater, Romaine & Christie on account of his loss of memory. That while in the service he <u>always served as a private</u>. That all his services were in the <u>militia</u> in the State of New Jersey & that according to the best of his recollection he was drafted at all of his terms of service except the year that he served under Captain Demarest. That his services were confined to the State of New Jersey & that he was not put under the command of the officers of the Regular troops at all & that he was in no particular engagement except the one in which he was wounded as above stated. That he has no documentary evidence of his services except the affidavit of Captain Demarest…& that he knows of no other person whose testimony he can procure who can testify to his service. He would however refer the Secretary of War to the fact of his being at present an Invalid Pensioner on the New York Roll & has drawn his pension since August 1806 & that his name is not on the Pension Roll of the Agency of any other state than the said State of New York & that he relinquishes all claims to a pension except the present & the Invalid Pension. That the clergyman in his parish has but lately moved into the place & he is totally unacquainted with him & he has therefore procured the attendance of Edward C. Reed & Moses B. Butterfield two residents of the town of Homer who can testify to his character for veracity & their belief of his services as a soldier of the revolution & to his age.

CHAPTER 8

PETER DEY

Preakness

In what is now Passaic County, and 235 years ago the western edge of Bergen County in the area known as Preakness, lay the beautiful stone and brick mansion of Colonel Theunis Dey, commanding officer of the county's militia. By 1774, Dey was a member of the Provincial Assembly and a prominent Whig in the county. His brother Richard, also of Preakness, would likewise serve early in the conflict as a major in the militia. The subject of this profile is Peter Dey, son of the colonel, who was a lad of fifteen years when the conflict arrived in Bergen County in 1776.

Amongst the incidents related by Dey was a "friendly fire" incident near the Paramus Church, one that resulted in the death of at least one soldier of the Fourth Battalion, New Jersey Volunteers, Garret Lockwood. The expedition consisted of three hundred New Jersey Volunteers, under the command of Lieutenant Colonel Joseph Barton of the Fifth Battalion, attempting to attack a force of militia at Pompton under Brigadier General Nathaniel Heard. In their way was the "Ranger Company" of militia under Captain Fell, in which was serving sixteen-year-old private Peter Dey. The incident was related to George Washington by Heard on May 14, 1777:

The new recruits from Bergen under the command of Colonels Barton & Buskirk, came up to Paramus with about 300 men with an intent to surprise the detachment I had there, about 70 men under the command of Captains Fell & *[Ebenezer]* Berry. The Enemy arrived there about the break of day and surround*[ed]* the house our men had quartered at the day before, but fortunately, Captain Fell who had received some information of some of them being seen at Hackensack the evening before, prudently moved their quarters about ten o'clock at night or they certainly must have fallen into the enemy's hands. The morning being somewhat hazy by which the enemy could not know their own men and suppose not rightly consulting each other of any signal, they began a very warm fire at each other and continued some time & Captain Fell's men still on their backs firing away put them in some confusion and am informed made Colonel Barton tremble and swear they would be all cut off for the Rebels had entirely surrounded them, when at the same time it was his own men. Day light appearing they with shame found the error they had committed, and immediately collected in a body and marched off.

Another incident in which Dey makes some reference, is one previously touched on in the declaration of David Ritzema Bogert, namely that of the militia being used by the sheriff of the county, Adam Boyd, to serve a writ on the quartermaster of Baylor's Dragoons in September 1778, shortly before their defeat at the hands of the British Light Infantry. While the incident made an impression on the inhabitants of Bergen, Baylor for his part viewed it as a nuisance, sending a captain off from Hackensack to Washington on September 22 "for the relation of an affray that has happened here between the civil authority and Major [Alexander] Clough; my motives for troubling you with this dispute is that complaints have been made to the governor who will probably make them known to you."

Baylor was even more dismissive the following day, following the attempted arrest of his men, coupled with the British arrival in the county, writing from Hackensack to Washington: "A Regiment of Militia which were here last evening to assist the sheriff in taking two of my men prisoners deserted us, as soon as this news was heard, the colonel himself could not be prevailed on to stay." The colonel would have been Peter Dey's father, Theunis.

Dey would serve the remainder of the war, being promoted to sergeant along the way. He would take part in hard fighting against Thomas Ward's Refugees, particularly at Bull's Ferry in 1780 and Fort Lee the following year. Even though Peter Dey would move to upstate New York after the war, his father's mansion still stands today, as an important historic site in Wayne, maintained by the Passaic County Parks Department. His pension application is No. S15078.

On this fifth day of February in the year 1834 personally appeared in open court before the judges of the Court of Common Pleas in the County of Seneca now sitting, being a court of record, Peter Dey a resident of the Town of Seneca Falls in the County of Seneca & State of New York, aged seventy three years; who being first duly sworn according to law in open

The area of Paramus Church figured in several engagements during the war, including Peter Dey's action against the New Jersey Volunteers in May 1777. *Courtesy of Todd W. Braisted.*

court doth on his oath make the following declaration, in order to obtain the benefit of the Act of Congress passed June 7th 1832.

That he entered the service of the United States under the following named officers and served as herein Stated.

On the twenty second day of August in the year one thousand seven hundred & seventy six he was ordered out into actual service under Captain Crines Van Houten and marched from his residence in the Town of Saddle River in Bergen County, New Jersey to Elizabeth Town Point, remained there ten or fifteen days; and then was ordered to Bergen Heights and remained there the remnant of the time, being one month in actual service as a private soldier. The colonel's name was Theunis Dey, the father of this declarant. He was the colonel at home of the whole regiment and on this tour commanded in person the detachment, except a part of the time was absent at Trenton as member of the legislature. He went to give his vote for William Livingston for governor, the first governor ever elected by the people of New Jersey and the first time Livingston was elected.

In the year 1777 about the 27th of April he volunteered as a private into a company of rangers and went into actual service under Captain Peter Fell, Joost Zabriskie 1st Lieutenant, John Van Allen 2nd Lieutenant & *[torn]*. During this tour I marched from Saddle River to Paramus *[torn]* head quarters were established. This company marched a great deal, ranged all the lower part of the County of Bergen, marched to Hoboken, several times to Fort Lee and to other places, to protect the country from the incursions of the Tories. Had no particular field officers, the company officers were commissioned or appointed by the colonel, Theunis Dey. General *[Nathaniel]* Heard lay at Pompton with some troops & sometimes reinforced us with a few men, all however commanded by our Captain Fell. We had a battle with the Refugees at Paramus, that time, in May. Joseph Barton commanded the Refugees. They surrounded Mrs. Hopper's house and fired upon one another, whilst our company lay some ways off. We then attacked them and drove them. The deponent served in this tour one month and three days as a private.

The next August or September he the deponent was ordered out again (1777) and served as sergeant in the company commanded by Captain James Christie, Samuel Campbell, Lieutenant, lay at Schraalenburgh, & kept a company guard one month, during that time were out frequently on scouting parties; no field officers or other troops near our station.

In June 1778 was ordered out again & served as sergeant in a company commanded by Captain David Haring. Kept company guard at a place called Closter in Harrington, Bergen County one month. Abraham Perdun was lieutenant. No field officers near the station.

In June 1779 was ordered out again & served as sergeant under Captain Elias Romaine, Samuel Campbell Lieutenant, stationed at the Liberty Pole in the Town of Hackensack, on company guard, no field officers, served one month.

In September 1779 was ordered out & served as sergeant under the same Captain Elias Romaine, and the same Lieutenant Samuel Campbell, a company guard stationed at the same place, Liberty Pole Hackensack. Served one month this tour as sergeant, no field officers.

In last of September & 1st of October 1779 *[1778]* was ordered out again under Captain John Mead. The whole regiment was ordered out this time, on what was called the long alarm, Colonel Theunis Dey commanded, *[John]* Mauritius Goetschius was 2nd Major. Marched to Hackensack first, thence to Paramus, then back through Hackensack to Acquackanonk. There were four regiments out this time commanded by General *[William]* Winds, all militia. The regiment in which deponent served, commanded by his father Theunis Dey, was on the ground some days before General Winds came up. The Enemy had crossed a party over at Hoboken under Cornwallis & *[Major]* General *[Charles]* Grey & were marching up the river plundering & foraging. There were no Continental troops near but a regiment of horse under the command *[of]* Colonel *[George]* Baylor who kept 9 or 10 miles off. During this time Colonel Baylor moved his troops from Hackensack by us & went up to Old Tappan without consulting our officers. There was some ill will existing between Baylor's Corps and our militia on account of deponent's father being called upon to aid with his regiment the Sheriff of Bergen to serve civil process on Baylor's quartermaster & other officers for having taken citizen's cattle by force, at the home of one Aaron Schuyler. Baylor's Horse by this were placed for the night in barns at Old Tappan, which enabled General Grey to get between us and Baylor in the night and he murdered almost all of them asleep. Deponent served on this occasion three weeks as sergeant.

In May 1780 he was ordered out under *[Captain]* David Van Bussen, Henry Van Bryck Lieutenant & Abraham Post Ensign, was stationed at Hackensack, a company's guard, no field officers. Served as sergeant one month. During this tour deponent volunteered out of his company to go with eighteen others under Captain Thomas Blanch to patrol or search in the neighborhood of a blockhouse erected by the Tories on the margin of the Hudson River who kept a formidable force there, to get wood for the

A scene from the commemoration of the 225th anniversary of the 1778 British Grand Forage, held at Historic New Bridge Landing in 2003. *Courtesy of Susan Nabors Braisted.*

enemy at the City of New York out of Bergen Woods. These Tories who garrisoned this Blockhouse had committed a great many murders in Bergen & one in particular by the name of John Berry commonly called <u>Jack the regular</u> had committed thirteen murders in Bergen County & among them one man of eighty years old by the name of Allen. On the 3rd of June this deponent with Captain Blanch came upon this notorious murderer, Jack the regular, about two miles from the blockhouse & took two prisoners & killed Jack & two others & carried the body of Jack to Hackensack to show the people that their dangerous enemy was no more. Two months after this, General Anthony Wayne attacked this blockhouse, with the Continentals & got defeated. He lost on this occasion eighty two killed & wounded out of Colonel Jackson's Regiment Pennsylvania troops.

In July this year (1780) General Washington made his head quarters at deponent's father's house for four weeks. His private Secretary was Benjamin Harrison, His aides Alexander Hamilton, David Humphreys, Richard Kidder Meade & Tench Tilghman whilst at our house this time, William Colfax commanded the Life Guard, Major *[Caleb]* Gibbs was absent.

A few days after Major *[John]* André was hung Washington came back & took up his quarters again at our house & staid seven weeks. Left our house on the 27th November 1780.

In April & May 1781 deponent served a month as a sergeant in actual service under Capt. John Outwater as it was pronounced, probably spelled Oldwater. Stationed at Hackensack a company guard, Cornelius Stagg was Lieutenant, was no ensign this time. No field officers, or regular troops near.

In April according to the best of his recollection in the year 1782 *[1781]* he was ordered out with his whole company, the whole regiment under the command of his father Colonel Theunis Dey were detached & marched to

Fort Lee to drive away the Refugees who were rebuilding the old Fort (Lee) for a harbor, their old blockhouse in Bergen Woods having been burnt the year before. Was in a battle with the enemy, at the fort, cleared them out, & they never attempted to harbor again along the west side of Hudson river in Bergen County; served this time as a sergeant two weeks.

The deponent declares that he was in actual military service of the United States detached by order of his father Colonel Theunis Dey who was the legal commander of the regiment to which deponent belonged, in all the times of service above related, with his company when called out in a body, and in his turn when his class had served—except one tour above stated he volunteered 1 month & 3 days under Captain Fell, to join a company of rangers, which company was not under the usual military organization, but was recognized as in the military service of the country and was duly appointed by Colonel Dey.

When declarant entered the militia service as above stated he resided with his father Colonel Theunis Dey in the Township of Saddle River in the County of Bergen & State of New Jersey & resided there and formed part of his father's family during the whole Revolutionary War except when he was in service. Has no record of his age. Since the year 1801 he has resided in the town of Fayette in the County of Seneca & State of New York until the two last years, during which he has resided in the Town of Seneca Falls in said county.

Has never received any written discharge from the service, and has no documentary evidence.

David Dey the brother of the declarant of the town of Varick in the County of Seneca & State of New York is a witness to the declarant's services & served with him a part of the time.

All the judges of this honorable court are well acquainted with the declarant and can testify to his credibility, as is also the Rev. Aaron D. Lane minister of the Presbyterian Church in this Town of Waterloo in said County.

He hereby relinquishes every claim whatever to a pension or annuity except the present and he declares his name is not on the pension roll of any agency in any state.

CHAPTER 9

EDWARD AND JUSTUS EARLE

Hackensack Township

*E*dward and Justus Earle were brothers living on their late father's land in Hackensack Township at the commencement of the war. Born in 1757 and 1749, respectively, these Loyalists were both early on commissioned officers in the Fourth Battalion, New Jersey Volunteers under Lieutenant Colonel Abraham Van Buskirk.

Edward Earle was commissioned lieutenant in the battalion on November 23, 1776; on the resignation of Peter Rutan, Earle was promoted to the captaincy of that company on July 3, 1781. As a lieutenant, Earle was involved in a number of actions during the war. On November 27, 1777, Earle, along with Lieutenant Jacob Van Buskirk (son of Abraham Van Buskirk) and Surgeon John Hammell, all of the Fourth Battalion, were made prisoners on Staten Island by a force of over 1,400 New Jersey Militia (including a company from Bergen County) under the command of Major General Philemon Dickinson. Loyalists taken prisoner by the Continental army were generally treated as prisoners of war, eligible for exchange for a soldier of equal rank serving for the United States. Prisoners taken by the militia however, fell under the control of the state, and that generally was not a good situation for the captive. The New Jersey Gazette heralded their capture, mockingly stating they were members of "a battalion of about 200 banditti, collected in Bergen, who eat King George's beef and pork to very little purpose." Each officer was turned over by the militia to the state's Committee of Safety for close confinement and trial for the crime of high treason. As Governor William Livingston wrote to George Washington four days after the raid:

> General Dickinson has sent me two lieutenants, one surgeon & one
> commissary taken prisoners on Staten Island by a detachment of our

militia under his command. As we found them all to be subjects of this state who had joined the enemy since that offence was declared high treason by our law, I have sent them to Trenton Jail to be tried in the County of Hunterdon, where a Court of Oyer & Terminer is to be held about the middle of this month.

Washington however, realized that states trying officers holding commissions from the British, even though they may have been residents of that state, could easily lead to reprisals by the British. Indeed, British Brigadier General John Campbell, commanding on Staten Island, wrote to Livingston that he had been informed the Loyalist officers were confined in a common jail like felons, and if such was the case "officers of equal rank, who were taken on this island the 22nd Day of August last, may be selected to undergo like treatment, however repugnant to the humanity of Britons to inflict it." All things considered, Washington wrote to the governor on December 11, giving his official opinion on the subject:

In my opinion, trying the officers, taken by General Dickinson on Staten Island, for high treason, may prove a dangerous expedient. It is true they left the state after such an offence was declared treason; but as they had not taken the oaths, nor had entered into our service, it will be said they had a right to choose their side. Again, by the same rule that we try them, may not the enemy try any natural born subject of Great Britain, taken in arms in our service? We have a great number of them, and I therefore, think we had better submit to the necessity of treating a few individuals, who may really deserve a severer fate, as Prisoners of War, than run the Risk of giving an opening for retaliation upon the Europeans in our service.

Livingston had no choice but to acquiesce, turning Earle and the others over to the commissary of prisoners, who promptly threw them into "close confinement" in retaliation of like treatment of some officers held by the British. A general exchange of prisoners put an end to the situation, which was effected in the summer of 1778.

Justus (or Joost) Earle would have his own experience as a guest of the United States, though not to the same degree as his brother. Justus was commissioned April 14, 1777, an ensign in the Fourth Battalion, serving with the unit until the early morning of August 19, 1779, when 400 troops under Major Henry Lee stormed an undermanned Paulus Hook. Ensign Earle, along with 4 other officers and 47 enlisted New Jersey Volunteers were taken *prisoner, amongst the 150 or so made captive by Lee that night. While the enlisted men were initially imprisoned in the cramped Philadelphia Jail (see Richard Wannamaker), the officers were allowed their parole. Officers signing a parole, either to the United States or the King, were typically free to roam within certain boundaries, in some cases a number of miles, from the place of their confinement. As for the confinement itself, it was typically a resident's house, with a few other officers, enjoying some creature comforts. A house in Pennsylvania that boarded several British officers of the Seventeenth Regiment of Foot who had been taken prisoner at Stony Point in 1779 enjoyed playing music, reading and even hunting while on parole. Earle, along with the other officers, would be exchanged in the large cartel between the two armies at the end of 1780.*

With their property confiscated, Edward and Justus would settle with other members of the battalion on grants of land given by the British in what is now the Province of New Brunswick, Canada. Justus Earle would live in Queen's County, New Brunswick, until he passed away on September 21, 1825. His brother Edward would eventually return to the new United States, dying in New York City on July 25, 1825. They had received from the British £500. on their claim of over £1,750. in property losses. Their memorials are in the TNA's AO 12/16/103-105.

The Memorial of Captain Edward Earle late of the Province of New Jersey Humbly Sheweth,

That in November 1776 your memorialist was on account of his loyalty obliged to quit his estate and home in New Jersey and take shelter within the King's Lines where he was honored with a commission and served until the peace when he came with the regiment to which he belonged to the River Saint John where he has resided ever since.

That he was with his Brother Lieutenant Justus Earle entitled to 139¾ acres of land with an house, barn & outhouses thereon situate in the County of Bergen & Precinct of Hackensack in the said Province of New Jersey in their own possession valued at £ 1746. 17. 6. New York Currency. Also 36¼ acres of land in the same place valued at £ 376 like money. 23 1/10 acres valued at £ 288. 5. like money. One acre of land with an house valued £ 87. 17. 6. all which have been seized and confiscated by the Rebels on account of your memorialist and his brother's loyalty.

That your memorialist and his said brother have also lost in like manner stock, farming utensils, grain, household furniture, wearing apparel and a riding chair valued together at £ 612. 12. like currency all which he humbly submits in full confidence of receiving such compensation and reimbursement as shall be just.

The beautiful silver sword-belt plate of Lieutenant Justus Earle. Made in New York City by the preeminent silversmith Lewis Fueter, this was a battalion design, showing the Royal Cipher, owner's initials and battalion motto *Amor Excitat Patriae* (excited by love of one's country). *Courtesy of the New Brunswick Museum, Saint John, N.B. Accession 2006.1.*

Evidence on the claim of Captain Edward Earle late of New Jersey.

Claimant Sworn

Saith he came to this province in October 1783, went up the River to Fredericton, sent his claim by Hardy, the claim was delivered here by his brother who continued in this town. He is a native of America, resided in Hackensack when troubles broke out. Joined the British in 1776, when Lord Cornwallis just came into the Jerseys.

Had a commission as lieutenant in [Lieutenant] Colonel Buskirk's [Regiment], afterwards had a captain's commission in same regiment. Has now half pay, served all the war, [and] is settled on the Grand Lake, Queen's County.

Claimant and his Brother Justus were in possession jointly of a farm in Hackensack. It was left to them two jointly by their father's will.

His father has been dead near 20 years. The land was not divided, [the] claimant being under age, so that it continued jointly in possession of the two brothers. It consisted of about 200 acres and upwards, there was a good house and barn. The elder Brother Justus was in possession of the whole.

Produces probate of his father's will, whereby his Father Silvester Earle gives Justus Earle & claimant the plantation in which he lived, equally to them and their heirs, paying £300 when claimant Edward came of age to three Daughters of Testators. Will dated in 1768, his father died soon after.

Produces copy of judgment against claimant, confiscating his estate with valuation by two appraisers at £2000 [New] York Currency.

Evidence on the claim of Justus Earle
late of New Jersey.

Claimant Sworn

Saith he is brother to Edward Earle. The claim is entered in both their names. The landed estate belonged to them equally. The moveable estate belonged to claimant.

Says he gave his claim to Mr. Hardy before Mr. Hardy went to Halifax. He gave it in the joint name of himself and brother.

Claimant lived at Hackensack, joined the British on their first coming to the Jerseys. Served first as a volunteer. In April *[1777]* had a commission as ensign in *[Lieutenant]* Colonel Buskirk's Regiment, had afterwards a commission as lieutenant. Continued to serve during the war. Has now half pay. Lives in Queen's County.

CHAPTER 10

ADAM, GEORGE, HENRY AND JACOB HAMEON

Masonicas

*T*he Hameon family of Masonicas (the Ramapo area) contributed five members to the Loyalist cause: the four whose memorials are here and a fifth, Nicholas, who served the whole war and likewise settled in Shelburne afterwards but apparently filed no claim. The Jacob Hameon who served through the war in the New Jersey Volunteers passed away shortly after the corps was disbanded in 1783 along the River Saint John; his claim, therefore, was filed by his son and heir of the same name.

Several aspects of Adam Hameon's story are confusing at best, particularly his enlistment in the Continental army. The muster roll of Captain John Maxwell's Company of Colonel Oliver Spencer's Additional Regiment shows Hameon enlisted in that corps on February 15, 1777, and deserting on May 1 of the same year. Of even more interest though, is that several other members of the Fourth Battalion, New Jersey Volunteers both enlisted with him on the same date and likewise deserted with him on the same date, namely, Samuel Bond, Conrad Wrap and Philip Young. Bond was a soldier in Major Timpany's Company, while the other two served with Hameon in Captain Rutan's Company. It is highly unlikely this was a coincidence, but the actual story behind this action may never be known. Wrap and Young are both listed as having been discharged in 1777, while Bond returned and continued in the Volunteers. In any instance, Adam was listed as a deserter from the Volunteers in 1777, then two months later in the General Hospital at New York City, where he remained until that summer until officially listed as on furlough, after which he is dropped from the rolls.

George Hameon appears to have served through the war without incident. He may have been a carpenter in civilian life, as he was employed as such on Staten Island to build a store, probably a storehouse for the battalion. Henry Hameon's service in the Volunteers ended in

1777, when health no longer permitted active service in the army. He did serve afterward, however, as a laborer at Marston's Wharf in the Commissary General's Department, one of the civil branches of the army. The civil branches performed most of the logistic services of the British Army, from driving wagons to cutting wood to issuing provisions to anything else needed to support the military. They provided literally thousands of Loyalists throughout America a means of support, particularly those not suited for the hardships of a soldier's life. While the battalion to which George and Jacob (and Nicholas) belonged was disbanded on October 10, 1783, in what is now New Brunswick, Canada, Adam and Henry initially settled in Shelburne, Nova Scotia, coincidently where Abraham Van Buskirk himself would settle. Shelburne would swell rapidly in size to one of the largest cities in North America and almost just as rapidly decrease in size as Loyalist refugees moved off to the countryside in hopes of better prospects in making new lives. Their claims for compensation are in AO 13/25/229-242.

The Memorial of Adam Hameon a Loyalist from the Province of New Jersey humbly sheweth

That your memorialist at the commencement of the late rebellion resided at Masonicas in the County of Bergen and Province of New Jersey. That his loyalty to his sovereign and attachment to the British Government induced him to embrace the earliest opportunity to get within the British lines; accordingly he joined the British troops in the year 1776, where he enlisted [as] a common soldier in the Fourth Battalion of New Jersey Volunteers, commanded by Lieutenant Colonel Abraham Buskirk when the British was at Hackensack in which he served faithfully for the space of nine months, in which time I was sent out by Major [Daniel Isaac] Browne which was a recruiting officer in order to fetch in some recruits, but unhappily he was taken by the Rebels and was obliged to enlist out of confinement rather than to wait for an exchange, on condition that he got a pass to go to his place for fifteen days and then instead of joining the Rebels he made his escape to His Majesty's troops again; then after some time he got liberty to go to the country to see his family, before he was five miles from the British lines he was taken again and was put immediately in irons and was marched to Lancaster with two other prisoners chained to me for four weeks, after which I was set at liberty by order of General Washington which order was granted through the request of an officer, which officer had agreed with his wife to clear him for the choice of his horses which his wife gave him, then he returned to his place where he stayed two days then he was taken again and made his escape again and crossing the lines he was so misfortunate as to receive a wound but made his escape and got in to the British lines and after

The Hameon family in 1777 would have appeared very much like these reenactors from the Fourth Battalion, New Jersey Volunteers. All Provincial forces raised during that campaign would receive a distinctive green coat faced white, earning them the nickname "The Greens." *Courtesy of Todd W. Braisted.*

his wound was cured *[the]* then Governor *[James]* Robertson cleared him from the regiment and put him in the Commissary General's Department, where he served till the immigration of the Loyalists into Nova Scotia.

As your memorialist will not appear at the presentation of this therefore prays his claim may be lodged and his case taken in consideration as early as possible and that under your report he may be enabled to receive such aid and relief as his loss may be found to deserve and am in duty bound will ever pray

The Memorial of George Hameon a Loyalist from the Province of New Jersey humbly sheweth

That your memorialist at the commencement of the late rebellion, resided at Masonicas in the County of Bergen & Province of New Jersey. That his loyalty to his sovereign, and attachment to the British government induced him to embrace the earliest opportunity to get within the British lines. He joined the King's troops in the year 1776 when they came to Hackensack where he enlisted *[as]* a common soldier in the 4th Battalion of New Jersey

Volunteers commanded by Lieutenant Colonel Abraham Buskirk where he served faithfully the full term of seven years, when he received his discharge from said regiment. That your memorialist left behind him both real and personal estate…which he could by no means bring off. As your memorialist will not appear at the presentation of this, therefore prays his claim may be lodged and his case taken into consideration as early as possible and that under your report he may be enabled to receive such aid and relief as his losses may be found to deserve. And as in duty bound he will ever pray.

The memorial of Henry Hameon a Loyalist from the Province of New Jersey humbly sheweth

That your memorialist at the commencement of the late rebellion, resided at Masonicas in the County of Bergen & Province of New Jersey. That his loyalty to his sovereign and attachment to the British government induced him to embrace the earliest opportunity to get within the British lines; he joined the King's troops in the year 1776 when they came to Hackensack where he enlisted a common soldier in the 4th Battalion of New Jersey Volunteers commanded by Lieutenant Colonel Abraham Buskirk, where he served six months then by reason of being much troubled with the Rheumatics and lameness he was found unfit for duty and was discharged; then as soon as he was able he entered in the forage yard under Commissary *[George]* Brinley where he served until the emigration of the Loyalists to Nova Scotia, then came to Shelburne. Your memorialist was unable to bring off with him the articles specified in the annexed schedule and upon his joining His Majesty's Troops they were taken, sold or otherwise disposed of by the Rebels. As your memorialist will not be present at the presentation of this, *[he]* therefore prays his claim may be lodged and his case taken in*[to]* consideration as early as possible, *[so]* under your report he may be enabled to receive such aid and relief as his losses may be found to deserve. And as in duty bound he will ever pray

The memorial of the heirs of Jacob Hameon Loyalist from the Province of New Jersey humbly sheweth

That your memorialists's father Jacob Hameon at the commencement of the late Rebellion resided at Masonicas in the County of Bergen and Province of New Jersey. That his loyalty to his sovereign and attachment to the British government induced him to embrace the earliest opportunity to get within the British lines; accordingly he joined the British troops in the year 1776 when they came to Hackensack, then he enlisted a common soldier in the

Henry Hameon's service in the civil branches of the army was common among Loyalists no longer fit for service in the ranks with a musket or who needed to support a family with something more than a common soldier's pay. Woodcutting, as shown here by these Loyalist reenactors at Fort Lee Historic Park, became a lucrative occupation for many Refugees. *Courtesy of Fort Lee Historic Park.*

4th Battalion of New Jersey Volunteers commanded by Lieutenant Colonel Abraham Buskirk, in which corps he served faithfully for and during the late Rebellion. When peace was proclaimed he went with the regiment to Saint John where he lived a few months, then your memorialists's father and mother both died within fourteen days of each other, then your memorialists being six in number fatherless and motherless in a strange and new country, having no relations near, they were much distressed, but having uncles in Shelburne that heard of their distress and sent a letter for them, then your memorialists came to Shelburne and now are living with their uncles. It was the desire of their father Jacob Hameon on his death bed that their Uncle Adam Hameon should take the charge of your memorialists and see that they get their father's rights. Accordingly, said Adam Hameon hath provided thus far for your memorialists, prays the said Adam Hameon may be accepted by the Honorable Commissioners as guardian for the children which are now your memorialists. That your memorialists being under age leaves this whole matter to their uncles to present their claims as they were personally acquainted with all our family's circumstances in regard of both character and estate. Your memorialists will not appear at the presentation of this, therefore prays their claim may be lodged and their case taken in consideration as early as possible and that under your report they may be enabled to receive such aid and relief as their loss may be found to deserve and am in duty bound will ever pray

CHAPTER 11

ELIAS AND CATRENA HOLMES

Hackensack Township

*E*lias Holmes was a free man of color in Bergen County, one of a large community of both enslaved and free blacks. While the British did not emancipate blacks at large, slavery being legal in England and the colonies, Sir Henry Clinton did extend such freedom to those who belonged to those who were enemies to Great Britain. This inducement, starting in 1779, led to a large exodus of escaped slaves into the British lines, so much so that it prompted a plea to Abraham Cuyler, commanding the blockhouse at Bull's Ferry on May 25, 1780, to halt forwarding them across the Hudson: "...not only the Male but Female Negroes with Children take advantage of your Post in New Jersey, to run away from Masters and come into this City, (which if they are suffered to do) they must become a burden to the Town..." The British Army being a white organization, blacks were left to find other means of employment or service, such as with the civil branches of the army, the Royal Navy, privateers or with the Refugees under Thomas Ward or King's Militia Volunteers. Elias Holmes utilized two of these opportunities, first by serving in the Quarter Master General's Department, attached as a wagoner to the Seventy-first Highlanders while they lay in Bergen County during December 1776 and then in arms under Captain Samuel Peek in the King's Militia Volunteers. In this latter service, he was extremely active, taking a number of prisoners in both Bergen and Orange Counties. At the end of the 1778 British Grand Forage, his luck ran out, traveling alone in the county "...in order to see his family in the country, and after being wounded in three different places, having his thigh-bone broken, by the Rebels, they in that condition cast him into prison at Hackensack which happened on the 15th day of October 1778, where he remained until the 10th of last May, when he broke prison along with three others, and by the help of crutches he came to New York where he has since remained." The jail break was immediately advertised by Sheriff

Adam Boyd, in an attempt to apprehend Holmes and the three other Loyalists who went off with him, describing him as "a mulatto, aged about 35 years, is lame in his left foot, about 5 feet 11 inches high. He was indicted for high treason at the court of this county." The reward on his head was sixty dollars, more than that offered for the return of the white Loyalists. He would successfully escape to New York, but his infirmities would render him—and by extension, his family—as objects of charity for the rest of the war. Unlike the majority of Loyalists who chose to settle in Nova Scotia, the Holmeses would opt for a new life in Quebec.

The memorial of Elias Holmes late of Hackensack, County of Bergen, State of New Jersey; but now of Sorel, in the Province of Canada, sheweth

That, from the unhappy rise of the late troubles in America, he was strongly attached into the British Constitution. That he adhered steadfastly to his allegiance, and exerted himself to the utmost of his ability, using his utmost endeavors to promote the interest of the British Nation. That he joined the British in 1776 at Fort Lee, and served in the Quarter Master General's Department, as may appear from the evidences and references of David Mathews Esqr., Oliver Bourdet, Major Robert Timpany, John Hicks Surgeon, all supposed to be in England or in Nova Scotia, Geores Haws of Sorel, Captain Maybee, Captain Latong, Gilbert Bogert all residing at the Bay of Quinte and others if required.

That in consequence thereof, your memorialist has truly been a great sufferer by being wounded in three different places, besides suffering many losses, a brief estimate of which is as follows, viz.

House, and furniture, Sterling	£13.	17.	0.
One horse and three cows	11.	18.	6.
One loom and tackling, book debts	10.	7.	0.
Cash taken from him by the Rebels £ 9. 9. Ditto by fines £ 6. 6.	15.	15.	0.
For arrearages still due for services in the Quarter Master General's Department from the 24th of January to the 2nd of June following at 6s/9d per day	43.	17.	6.
[Total]	£107.	15.	0.

The 2nd of June 1777, being wounded & taken prisoner and confined in jail for 2 years and ten days on his own expense during the whole of said time.

Errors Excepted

Your Memorialist therefore prays, that his case may be taken into consideration, in order that he may receive such compensation, which his losses and services, may be found to deserve.

During the war, Elias and his wife, Catrena, both suffered greatly on account of poverty. His wounds and their destitute state prompted Bergen County's Loyalist Refugee community in New York City to solicit aid on their behalf. The September 17 document is extremely valuable, detailing some of the prisoners taken by Refugees early in the war. Two of the men who assisted in the taking of Major Blauvelt and Harmanus Tallman were John King and Isaac Depue, who were later taken prisoner by the Rebels, tried by court-martial and sentenced to death. Both were pardoned by George Washington on July 4, 1779.

New York July the 20th 1779

I do hereby certify that the bearer Catrena Holmes has a husband now laying in the College Hospital wounded in three places by the Rebels so that it is not expected that he will in a year's time be able to do anything, and as the bearer is now come down with four small children and an old mother and has no way of living, it is therefore hoped they may be allowed to draw rations—

[Signed]

David Peek Captain
David Mathews
George Shaw
Wm. Franklin
Governor of New-Jersey

New York September the 17th 1779

We the subscribers do hereby certify that the bearer Elias Holmes has been a loyal subject from the beginning of this Rebellion and has done a great many services for government. In the first place he turned out with David Peek Captain in the King's Militia Volunteers which was in the year 1777, when he assisted in taking and bringing to the provost guard of this city one Captain Thomas Kennedy, a noted Rebel plunderer only with three of us; after that the noted Nathaniel Killy a Rebel commissary general; after

The civil branches, unlike the Regular Army and Provincial Corps, was an area where black and white Loyalists could serve side by side, hence Elias Holmes's tenure in the Quartermaster General's Department. *Courtesy of Fort Lee Historic Park.*

that Captain *[Caleb]* Bruen his brother *[Lieutenant Jeremiah Bruen]* and David Schuyler, noted Rebels and Rail Riders; after that Major *[Johannes Joseph]* Blauvelt *[and]* Harmanus Tallman; after that Isaac Blanch a committee man, Jacobus Blauvelt, Jacob Wortendyke and several others, and many other Rebel persecutors at different times until he got wounded by the Rebels in three places which has so disabled him that he is not able to help himself; he has likewise been confined by the Rebels in Hackensack Jail until the 10th of May last when he together with four of them broke jail and came to this city where he is now with his wife and four small children unable to Support *[themselves.]* He has likewise been a wagoner in His Majesty's Service from the 4th Day of December 1776 until the 23rd Day of January 1778, together with a wagon and horses for which he never received any pay; we therefore hope his case may be considered

Witness to the Above

David Peek Captain
Jacobus Peek
Charles Beekman
John Ryckman
Lawrence Van Buskirk Captain

N.B. the said Elias Holmes was born in Bergen County in the Province of East New Jersey where he has lost all his effects taken from him by the Rebels.

Finding no success, the Refugees once again petitioned to add the Holmes family to the provision list. This list was administered by the New York Loyalist colonel Roger Morris, a man almost universally detested by the Refugees for his parsimonious attitude in adding Loyalists to the government rolls.

These are to certify *[to]* whom it may concern that Elias Holmes entered into His Majesty's Service as a wagoner to the 71st Regiment under the command *[of]* Sir William Erskine the fourth of December 1776, having a wagon and two Horses of his own and on the 23rd day of February following he was discharged; after which he came to New York, from thence he went in order to see his family in the country, and after being wounded in three different places, having his thigh bone broken, by the Rebels, they in that condition cast him into prison at Hackensack which happened on the 15th day of October 1778, where he remained until the 10th of last May, when he broke prison along with three others, and by the help of crutches he came to New York where he has since remained.

The bearer along with two more have taken and brought into this city, the noted Rebel Captain *[Thomas]* Kennedy; which was the cause of his being so ill used by the Rebels. And we do farther certify that the bearer is a Loyal Subject to His Majesty King George, and for which he has lost his all, viz. house, lands & movables, such as his clothes, his grain etc. all which was taken from his poor wife when he lay in prison, and his poor wife and four small children sent away almost naked to this city etc. Given under our hands in New York this 29th day of November 1779.

Samuel Peek Captain
Jacobus Peek
John Ryckman

I have enquired into the circumstances set forth in the above certificate, and have reason to believe them true, and do therefore recommend the said Elias Holmes to His Excellency the Commander in Chief for relief & assistance.

William Franklin
Governor of New Jersey

CHAPTER 12

JAMES AND CATHARINE KENT

Franklin Township

*O*ne of the more interesting residents of the war in Bergen County was a young James Kent. Kent served Congress in the militia and state troops and for almost three months served King George in the Fourth Battalion, New Jersey Volunteers. Kent passed away before the act of Congress providing pensions for veterans. His story was told by his widow, Catharine, whom he married during the war, while in service. Her relation of their courtship intermixed with his service splendidly shows that even in time of war, life in the county went on. Kent goes into detail of his service in the state troops while serving as a picket at New Bridge. New Bridge was the main crossing of the Hackensack River and a vital strategic point, important to the U.S. troops in protecting the interior country and to the British as their entry point to the same country. William Lozier, a friend of Kent's during the war, fondly recalled decades later "that he being acquainted with the said James Kent, could cross the bridge in the night by giving the said James Kent something to drink, which he recollects of having often done."

Kent was in service with Captain John Outwater's State Troops when three hundred British and German troops under Lieutenant Colonel Duncan McPherson of the Forty-second Highlanders appeared in Hackensack at 4:00 a.m. on March 23, 1780, in order to capture the militia and state troops who "were assembled to protect sundry new fangled Justices of the Peace, who had assembled there to devise means to harass and distress such of their neighbors as were thought to be disaffected to the cause of rebellion." Kent's capture was confirmed by the New-York Gazette and the Weekly Mercury, listing him amongst the dozens of men taken at Hackensack and Paramus that early morning. While Catharine Kent believed James had either been exchanged or enlisted with the British, he absolutely did the latter. And he almost certainly knew the people he enlisted with, having *signed on in Captain Jacob Van Buskirk's Company of the Fourth Battalion, New Jersey Volunteers, serving alongside Westervelts, Christies, Rykers, Allens and many other Bergen names. The roll of the company also shows he enlisted immediately after his capture, not after a period of prolonged despair as he may have told Catharine. There was no mistaking that he did desert from the Loyalists though, the rolls showing him as having absconded from Staten Island on June 1, 1780.*

Our blacksmith turned soldier's next service would be in the state troops. At this time in 1780, two state units were being formed in the county, one under Major John M. Goetschius and the other under Captain Thomas Blanch. Both these units were in service when the thirteen-thousand-man Continental army under Washington himself entered Bergen County that August, seeking provisions for the starving men and putting them in a position to cooperate with an anticipated French expeditionary force in an attack on British-held New York City. Kent eventually found himself serving under Captain Blanch, whom Washington personally tasked with guarding the passage up the Palisades that Cornwallis had taken in 1776 to capture Fort Lee. To Washington's astonishment, however, Blanch did not deploy his men, citing a lack of provisions and tents. Washington erupted on the citizen soldier captain, exclaiming, "I cannot help expressing exceeding great surprise at your not obeying the orders you received yesterday, to take post with the men under your command at the Closter landings. Nor do I see how you could have answered it to yourself and your Country, if any disaster had happened in consequence of your neglect."

One other notable occurrence during Kent's service was the execution at "Log Jail" of two of Abraham Van Buskirk's men, Noah Callaghan and John Van Iderstine. The rolls show both men had deserted the New Jersey Volunteers on September 19, 1782. Rivington's Royal Gazette *published an account of their execution, alluding it was on account of high treason. Callaghan had briefly served in the Third New Jersey Continentals before deserting to the British in March 1777. For their part, most militia veterans simply said the men were great villains.*

Be it known that on the twenty third day of October, eighteen hundred and forty four, before me the undersigned one of the aldermen of the City of New York, personally appeared, Catharine Kent, residing at No. 153 Houston Street, in the City, County and State foresaid, who being first duly sworn according to law doth on her oath make the following declaration in order to obtain the benefit of the provision made by the act of Congress passed July 4, 1836.

That she is the widow of James Kent, or as he sometimes spelt his name "Kint," who was a private and sergeant in the Revolutionary War in the militia and other troops of Bergen County, New Jersey. That her husband the aforesaid James Kent, was a native of Sussex County, New Jersey and was at the time of the breaking out of the Revolutionary War, an apprentice to John Freeland, at the blacksmithing business, at a place called the "Ponds" in Franklin Township, in Bergen County, in the same state. That the said John Freeland upon the breaking out of the war give up the blacksmithing business and her said husband having no employment entered the service in the militia, and served as a substitute, for persons residing in that part of the county. That she was but little acquainted with him before July of the year 1777, but recollects before that time he served a monthly tour in Captain *[Elias]* Romaine's Company at the Liberty Pole in the English Neighborhood, and a tour of six or seven weeks under a captain whose name she does not recollect stationed down at Amboy in both of which periods she believes he served as a substitute, and was either corporal or sergeant…

That in the wheat harvest in the month of July 1779, she became intimately acquainted with her said husband, as it was at the time that their courtship commenced and at that time she distinctly recollects he was in service as a sergeant, in a company of troops, that was then stationed in the Village of Hackensack, and was quartered in Wilson's old School House and was commanded by a captain from the lower part of the state, whose name she has forgotten, but the lieutenant's name as she distinctly recollects was *[Abraham]* Post. That said company had, as she understood, been raised in the different counties by enlistment for one campaign, and that it continued so stationed, until on or about the first of January ensuing, when their terms expired and they were then discharged, as she well remembers. That said company kept a picket guard at New Bridge, of which guard she distinctly recollects her said husband was every other day the officer, and that she distinctly recollects he continued to serve in said company until it was discharged. That it is her impression that said company's term for which it had been raised to serve was six months, and she distinctly recollects that it was in what was called the Hard Winter that said company was discharged; and she also recollects that her said husband received his pay in paper money about the time he was discharged, and that said company drew their regular rations and cooked them in the farm houses, and lived in the school house, six soldiers being in a mess. That she lived during the time said company laid there between the Village of Hackensack and New Bridge, where said company's picket guard was kept, on the main road and that she distinctly recollects seeing the said pickets pass and re-pass every night and morning during the whole time it laid there, and that she does not know to what regiment said company belonged, if it belonged to any, nor did she know the names of any of his comrades, as they were all strangers in them parts, having come as she understood from the lower counties of the state.

That immediately after the above stated discharge of her said husband, he went up to the Ponds and failing to get any employment there, he came back to Hackensack again while yet it was winter, and she think it was Captain *[John]* Outwater, was then enlisting a company for three months service into whose company her said husband enlisted as sergeant for the term, and whether it was before, or just after said company had been embodied in to service she cannot remember, he was taken prisoner, and was taken to New York City, where he was kept a prisoner of war, until in June, when he, "as he, and others that was prisoners with him, afterwards informed her," despairing of being soon exchanged he enlisted with the enemy, and he was with the British Army sent down to Staten Island, where he deserted, and as she distinctly recollects he came to Hackensack in that same month dressed in a full suit of British regimentals. That he said he had been enlisted about one week when he deserted, and that his exchange had been effected by Captain *[John]* Willis a day or two before he came back, at which time the company in which he had enlisted had some time before served out their time and was discharged.

That immediately after his above stated return home in the month of June 1780, he enlisted as a sergeant with the Wars Men, in the Standing Army, for six months. She believes he enlisted in the regiment to which Major *[John Mauritius]* Goetschius belonged, for he came along a day or two after he had enlisted, and asked him why he was not at his post. That at the time he enlisted with the war men, for six months, Captain *[Thomas]* Blanch of the County of Bergen was enlisting a company of troops for a like period of six months, and a sergeant that had enlisted, in Captain Blanch's Company, whose name she does not recollect, and her said husband made an exchange and her said husband instead of serving with the <u>wars men</u> entered Captain Blanch's Company, which was embodied into service at Closter, on or about the first day of July for she well remembers that the period was for six months and that it, as she well remembers terminated on the firs[t] day of January, ensuing. That Captain James Christie, of the said County of Bergen paid her said husband his bounty for his enlistment, in gold in September, after his enlistment. That he served his full term of enlistment in Capt. Blanch's Company as sergeant. That said company of Captain Blanch when they were first embodied into service, laid for a short time in Closter Mountain, and was afterwards stationed at Closter, and the men were billeted in the farm houses. That soon after he entered upon

A typical guard room on either side would have included materials for orderly sergeants acting as clerks or amusements for soldiers waiting their turns as sentries. *Courtesy of Todd W. Braisted.*

his service in Blanch's Company he went up in Closter Mountains as a guide to show General *[Anthony]* Wayne the way to a block house, occupied by the Refugees, which General Wayne with the army attempted to take but did not succeed. That on Saturday the 23rd day of September, he got a furlough, and came down to Hackensack, and on Monday they were married, and on Tuesday he returned to his duty again, in Capt. Blanch's Company, and did not come down but once afterwards, until the first of January when he was discharged. That she recollects that he received his pay for that service but who paid him, or when, or in what kind of money she does not recollect.

That immediately after the termination of his service in Captain Blanch's Company in the same winter, they moved up to the Ponds in the said County of Bergen, and hired a house of John Tice, and went to housekeeping, and in March, it came his turn, to serve his month, but she expecting daily to be confined, with her first child, he was excused, and did not go, he was then at

A New Bridge romance developed between Catharine and James Kent during his tours of service on guard duty during the war. Despite the years of war, many aspects of normal life continued, such as weddings and baptisms. *Courtesy of Todd W. Braisted.*

work at his trade. Soon after which there was an alarm, and he went down to Hackensack, as a private in Captain Willis' Company he was only out two or three days. That she thinks it was in the fall of that year 1781 *[1782]*, there was a refugee confined in the Log Jail, at the place where they lived, by the name of Noah Callag*[h]*an, and a jail guard was called out, to guard the jail. Said jail guard was commanded by Captain Willis, and that her husband served as a private in the said jail guard from the time it was raised until the day the said Noah Callaghan was hung which was she thinks a few days short of a month, but it was understood that such service should be counted as a monthly tour. That he rendered no service of a military character after the day that the said Noah Callaghan was hung…That she should have made earlier application for a pension but she was informed, that her husband's enlistment with the enemy cut her off. That her maiden name was Catharine Parlaman, and that she was brought up in the family of Abraham Brower, who lived near New Bridge, with whom she continued to reside after her marriage, until the expiration of her said husband's above stated service under Captain Blanch. That they were married by the Reverend Mr. *[Dirck]* Romine of Hackensack at his house. That she is now aged eighty six years and upwards. That they lived at the Ponds as above stated, until about the year 1800, when they moved to the City of New York, where he soon after died, and she has ever since continued to reside, in said city. That she has no documentary evidence of the Revolutionary services of her said late husband nor does she know of the existence of any…

She further declares that she was married to the said James Kent on the twenty fifth day of September, in the year seventeen hundred and eighty, and that her husband the aforesaid James Kent, died July the 16th A.D. 1805, and that she has remained a widow ever since that period as will more fully appear, by reference to the proof hereunto annexed.

CHAPTER 13

ISAAC AND RACHEL NOBLE

Ramapo

*T*he war affected the men and women of both sides, as clearly demonstrated by this Loyalist husband and wife from Ramapo. Situated in a good Bergen County stone house on seventy-six acres of land, Isaac Noble left his home and family behind as soon as Lord Cornwallis entered the county in November 1776. Arriving at New Bridge, he met Brigadier General Cortland Skinner, commanding officer of the New Jersey Volunteers, who immediately set Noble about organizing recruits, telling him "Let the people know now is the time to evince their Loyalty by actions, not words." Moving out from New Bridge, he led Lieutenant Colonel the Honorable William Harcourt and a detachment of Sixteenth Light Dragoons to a ford on the Passaic River, enabling them to come behind Continental and militia forces covering Washington's retreat. It was shortly after this that he was grievously wounded, putting an end to any future prospects as an officer. After recovering sufficiently, he served as an assistant commissary at Marston's Wharf in Manhattan until waylaid and murdered in May 1779 by highwaymen, somewhere between the city and Kingsbridge.

Rachel Noble, like many spouses of Loyalist soldiers, was initially left at home to tend to the family and homestead until her husband returned. No one figured on a war that would last years or property confiscations. After a terrifying flight to the city with one of their children, Rachel spent over a year trying to reunite with her remaining children. Upon their arrival in the city, she immediately set sail with them for London, where, after the war, she filed a claim for the loss of their home and property, for which she received £400 and an annual pension of £80 through 1804. The Noble claim for losses is in Audit Office 13/110/351-353.

The Memorial of Rachel Noble in behalf of herself and four children humbly sheweth

That her late husband Mr. Isaac Noble of Ramapo in the County of Bergen in New Jersey, showed himself on every occasion a zealous assertor of the British Government, and endeavored to promote those sentiments wherever his influence extended, which was great among the German inhabitants from his knowledge of the language, and by which means he raised a number of Men who joined Brigadier General Skinner's corps.

When the Kings Troops entered New Jersey in the year 1776 Mr. Noble joined them at great hazard, and with a small party of Light Dragoons went a volunteer to reconnoiter the bridge at Acquackanonk which they found destroyed by the Rebels. He then offered himself a guide to ford the river at the head of a detachment in the face of the enemy posted on the opposite height, which he performed to the satisfaction of the commanding general. A regiment of Loyalists being ordered to be formed in New Jersey, Mr. Noble (in consideration of his zeal and services) had the honor of being named as major to the battalion commanded by [Lieutenant] Colonel [Abraham] Buskirk, and as appears by an order of General [Cortland] Skinner's, was going on duty as such, when he was attacked by a skulking party of Rebels near the camp at Acquackanonk and left by them as dead, having received a violent contusion on the head, and the thrust of a bayonet in the eye which was thereby totally lost. On the retreat of the King's Forces, he was in this lamentable condition conveyed to New York, where for many months he was under the care of Doctor [Michael] Morris. The wounds having affected the brain, he was near 18 months watched and treated accordingly, and his commission of major was of course never issued. During this calamity your memorialist suffered much ill treatment from her neighbors who were disaffected to government. She was informed of their resolution to take her into custody, which to avoid she fled by favor of a dark night, with an infant of nine months at her breast, on foot and unprotected, she suffered every thing which can be felt from terror, inclemency of weather, want of food and of every conveniency, by which her health was much impaired. Finding the impossibility of escaping with more than the infant at her breast, was obliged to leave three others to the mercy of the Rebels, who took them the day after their mothers escape, and stripped them of every thing necessary to their infant state even to their clothes, at the same time pillaged the house and farm of every thing portable, and destroyed what they could not carry away. The children remained prisoners near 13 months, at the

Isaac Noble's first task was to gather men for the New Jersey Volunteers and arrange them at New Bridge. Here, these corporals from the re-created Fourth Battalion, New Jersey Volunteers educate visitors to Historic New Bridge Landing in the intricacies of eighteenth-century weapons. *Courtesy of Todd W. Braisted.*

expiration of which time a flag *[of truce]* was obtained from his Excellency General *[Sir Henry]* Clinton to bring them to their parents at New York, which was done at great expense.

At Mr. Noble's recovery, finding himself totally ruined and destitute; the late Daniel Chamier Esqr. Commissary General, appointed him a Deputy Commissary for Provision and Forage, in which Department he gave satisfaction to the end of his life, which finally paid the forfeit of his attachment to his King and Country, being seized & murdered by a party of Rebels on his way to Kingsbridge upon duty; so obnoxious was Mr. Noble to the Rebels, that they promised a reward of 500 Dollars to any who should take or destroy him. His integrity in office is evident by the indigent situation in which he left his family, his widow and four children having nothing to subsist upon, but what they now receive by the bounty of government. Your memorialist came to England in February 1780 with her children, they

Wood was the primary fuel of the eighteenth century, in addition to being a valuable building material. Many of the trees in each town today would have been mostly cleared for farmland and use by the time of the Revolution. *Courtesy of Fort Lee Historic Park.*

were supported by the benevolence of her brother in law till April 1781 when death deprived her of so good a friend, since which time she has been considered a real object of the public munificence, and granted the sum of £100 per annum which is at present her whole support. Your memorialist therefore prays that her melancholy case may be taken into consideration in order that she may be enabled under your report to receive such aid or relief as her afflicting losses, sufferings, and her late husband's services may be found to deserve.

This document, attached to the above memorial, was entitled "Copy of a Memorandum of Mr. Isaac Nobles, made a short time before his Death, which ascertains in a great degree the amount of his Property etc."

Soldiers and Residents in Their Own Words

Memorandum

Not being bred to arms, I stayed in New Jersey about 30 miles from New York, till the troops entered it, when I immediately abandoned my family, house & home and joined the King's Army. The reason of first staying was to serve the Crown by opposing as far as in me lay, by my example (having some Interest in the country) the steps by which the Rebels undermined and gained the well affected, but mostly ignorant inhabitants, which first caused a prohibition of intercourse from the leaders; afterwards my being by night by express orders of their Government disarmed, and at last quitting them on the entering of the King's Troops having joined them, when they in a few hours must have taken me, by a party of Continental Troops who had been destroying all my moveable property to the amount of about fifteen hundred pounds currency, taken possession of my real estate, and offering even a sum for my head. When I had joined the troops, I offered my services, and was by Brigadier General Skinner offered a majority in the New Jersey Volunteers, and should have as I am fully persuaded, in a short time largely contributed to complete the battalion I was appointed to, had the army not left the country so soon after entering it. I after two days march with the army, by unknown persons in the skirts of the army, by a musket lost an eye, and health, by which I was for a twelve month rendered incapable of actual service, in which time another officer was appointed, and myself in order fully to recover and subsist a large family, served faithfully (by appointment of Mr. Chamier) in the Commissary Line as my accounts and the certificates I could collect from the troops I served fully show.

CHAPTER 14

ISAAC PERKINS

English Neighborhood

*O*ne of the most useful yet little-known Loyalists was Isaac Perkins. Born in North Castle, New York, Perkins had moved to English Neighborhood prior to the American Revolution, where he set up shop as a ferryman at the strategic Burdett's Landing, just below Fort Lee, also known as Fort Constitution. There he invested about £50 to purchase and operate a pettiauger, plying passengers and cargoes across the Hudson, then also known as the North River. The Burdett property, some of which he appeared to lease, provided an excellent vantage point to observe the fortifications and defenses going up around him in 1776. Indeed, Peter Burdett suffered immense loss from the establishment of Fort Lee, including crops, fence rails, timber, livestock and money stolen by soldiers in the garrison. It was at this time that Perkins performed the first of his two major services for the British, apparently. The situation was detailed by Captain Andrew Snape Hamond of the Royal Navy, commanding officer of HMS Roebuck:

> As the Rebel Army was chiefly supplied by the North River, and placed great dependence upon it, they had taken a great deal of pains to throw a boom across, by sinking vessels & frames of timber, to prevent our ships from passing up. They had placed these obstructions in the narrowest part, where the river is about 1200 yards wide, between two high lands, having Fort Washington on the right, and Fort Constitution [Lee] on the left, each containing several batteries of heavy cannon, placed at some distance along the shore, and six row galleys with each a large gun in their prow

guarded the boom in front; so that, we understood, they looked upon it to be perfectly secure: and it is possible, from seeing the great preparation they had made, we might also have thought so, if a deserter had not informed the admiral that there was a passage open between two of the sunken vessels (which his brother the ferry man had given him marks for) and offered himself as a pilot...

It is impossible to say whether this was a brother of Isaac Perkins or Peter Burdett, who was no Loyalist. That being said, it was most likely a brother of Isaac Perkins. The following day, October 9, 1776, the Royal Navy warships Phœnix, Rose *and* Tartar *sailed through the obstructions and past the forts "without the least obstruction and with but little loss." That loss consisted of nine men killed and twice that number wounded; amongst the latter was sixteen-year-old John MacGregor Skinner, son of Brigadier General Cortland Skinner, commanding officer of the New Jersey Volunteers, whose arm was shot off in the engagement. He would recover and advance through the ranks to end the war as a lieutenant in the Royal Navy.*

Perkins himself would perform a much more important piece of personal service that November 20. The previous evening, among the five thousand troops under Lord Cornwallis destined to cross the Hudson, was an order for "three guides." Perkins here identifies himself as one of those guides, his place of residence being no doubt of infinite benefit in qualifying him for that task. After the fall of the fort, Perkins himself would suffer loss, when his pettiauger, carrying captured stores from the fort, overset and sunk in the Hudson River. He then suffered further when the British took the hay from his leased land and other items. Perkins, unlike the Hameons and others who entered under Abraham Van Buskirk in the New Jersey Volunteers, did not enter into the Provincial service, choosing instead to work for a living and carry arms occasionally with Refugees on the other side of the Hudson. Despite his later serving under Colonel James DeLancey in his very active corps of Westchester County Militia and Refugees, Perkins was never able to recover the losses he suffered, and his claim was subsequently rejected. He arrived in Nova Scotia in May 1783 and some four years later was settled along the Kennebecasis River in New Brunswick.

The memorial of Isaac Perkins late of Hackensack & County of Bergen and Province of East New Jersey but now of the River St. John, Province of New Brunswick Humbly Sheweth

That whereas your memorialist was applied to by the agents of Congress in the year 1776 to sign a paper called the Association and on refusal of the same was Deemed an enemy to my country and committed

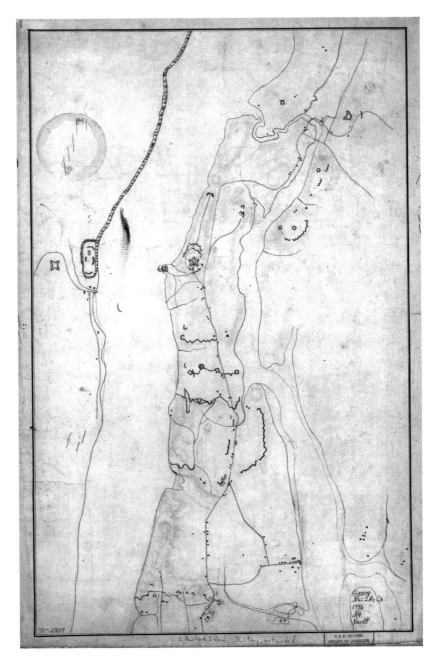

Forts Lee and Washington were strategically placed to deny the Royal Navy use of the Hudson River above Manhattan. Isaac Perkins, a ferryman on the river, was in a perfect position to observe the Rebel preparations and aid the British in passing the forts. *Courtesy of the Library of Congress, Washington, D.C.*

to close confinement from thence I found means to break prison and make my escape to the British Army and left my house, home and family to the mercy of my enemies to my loss and detriment. And when Lord Cornwallis marched across the North River I was his guide at Fort Lee from thence I bore arms under the command [of] James DeLancey commanding the Westchester Refugees during the whole war at my own expense voluntarily.

Therefore your honors' memorialist prays that your honors will take my sufferings and services into your consideration as in your great wisdom shall seem meet so that your memorialist may get redress in the premises and your honors memorialist as in duty bound shall ever pray.

An estimate of the loss of property sustained by Isaac Perkins, late of Hackensack in the County of Bergen, East New Jersey, for his attachment to the British Constitution.

November 1776

lost one pettiauger	£50.	0.	0.
One bateaux	5.	0.	0.
One pair two year old steers	7.	0.	0.
One calf	2.	0.	0.
One hog	3.	4.	0.
One horse saddle & bridle	15.	0.	0.
Fifty bushels of grain	7.	0.	0.
Household furniture & farming utensils	10.	0.	0.
Two tons of hay taken by the British	10.	0.	0.
	£109.	4.	0.
Reduced to Sterling at 75 the par of exchange	62.	8.	0.

CHAPTER 15

BENJAMIN ROMAINE

Hackensack Township

*A*mong the very finest of the U.S. pension applications is the lengthy account of *Benjamin Romaine. Romaine's story starts at the age of fourteen, when he describes his family fleeing in a boat across the Hudson while the attack on Fort Washington was underway. After entering the service in his mid-teens, Romaine took part in most of the major actions as a member of the Bergen County Militia. Most of his narrative is so well detailed that it requires little elaboration here. Two incidents, however, deserve further examination.*

The April 16, 1780 British raid on Hoppertown was directed at the detachment of 250 Continental troops posted there and was remarkably successful, despite the casualties suffered by the attackers. The militia, after the alarm was spread through the county, was mostly engaged in attacking the invaders on their retiring: the infantry to Fort Lee where they would embark and the cavalry to Bergen Point, and thence to Staten Island. His mention confronting the British & Loyalist cavalry in an open field must have been terrifying to Bergen's part-time soldiers. The account published in the April 19, 1780 edition of the Royal Gazette *spoke of the withdrawal in fairly bland terms:*

> In retiring, small parties of militia, with a few of their troops, who had been upon out duties, kept hovering round the detachment in different directions, and although unable to make any impression, they incommoded the march of the troops by a constant scattered fire from different quarters, but with little effect, although they continued their

attempts to the place of embarkation viz Fort Lee, at which the infantry arrived between 3 and 4 o'clock in the afternoon, the cavalry taking the same route by which they advanced; eight deserters with their arms joined the detachment early in the morning.

Of even more personal concern to Romaine was a little-heralded example of the petit-guerre that often took place in Bergen County, particularly during the period of 1780 to 1782 when Thomas Ward's Loyal Refugee Volunteers established their blockhouses on Bergen Neck. It also provides an excellent example of the civil war being waged, in this case neighbor against neighbor. Romaine's account differs in several respects from the account published by the British in the September 17, 1781 edition of the New-York Gazette and the Weekly Mercury, *which stated:*

> *On Wednesday evening last a party of Refugees, from Fort DeLancey, on Bergen Neck, consisting of only eleven men, under the command of Captain William Harding, made an excursion to Closter, in Jersey, being 25 miles from said post, where they surprised and made prisoners of a Rebel guard of six men, belonging to the noted Captain [Thomas] Blanch, and also collected fifteen head of cattle: all which they conducted with them back to Fort DeLancey, notwithstanding they were followed in their return for near twenty miles, by at least three times their number, under the command of a Colonel [Major] Goetschius, and the said Blanch, but without their venturing to make any attack, except now and then exchanging a few long shot at a very respectable distance.*

After Romaine's initial claim was rejected for want of time served, the frustrated veteran went to great lengths and admonitions in eventually proving his case. In addition to his time in the field, he also pointed out the clerical duties of being a sergeant, as fellow veteran Samuel Helm testified on his behalf in 1835, stating Romaine "was very ready with his pen in preparing muster rolls, pay rolls, regimental and company orders." Unlike many pension applications, which were transcribed by clerks listening to the veteran detail his experience in court, Romaine's is in the first person and appears to be a true narrative in his own words. His pension application in the National Archives is No. W18839.

On this twenty seventh day of May, one thousand eight hundred and thirty four, personally appeared before the Marine Court of the City of New York,

Benjamin Romaine, a resident of the City of New York, and in the County and State of New York, aged seventy one years, who, being first duly sworn, according to law, doth, on his oath, make the following declaration, in order to obtain the benefit of the provision made by the Act of Congress, passed June 7th 1832.

I was born near Poughkeepsie, Dutchess County, N.Y. on the twenty fourth day of September 1762. I have no record of my age: my father's Family Bible, in which the date was recorded, was lost. When I entered into the service, I was living near Hackensack, Bergen County, State of New Jersey, and since the Revolutionary War, I have lived in this City of New York, where I continue to reside.

In or about the month of August 1776 my father, mother and myself fled from this city to Fort Washington, a few miles above on the Hudson River. On the approach of the enemy, we crossed the Hudson to Fort Lee, on the opposite shore, while the cannon balls were flying over our heads, from Fort Lee, directed at the enemy's ships, which were endeavoring to ascend the river in aid of the storming Fort Washington: the capture of which fort was effected by them the next day or two thereafter. He became resident near Hackensack aforesaid and there, subsequently, continued to dwell, constantly however retreating from our home, on each advance of the enemy, and again returning to our desolated habitation, as they departed, for their stronghold, in this city. Such was the condition of all the Whig families, who remained faithful to their country's cause, during the Revolutionary War: they were captured and made prisoners of war, whether in actual service or not; while the Tory families staid at their homes, unmolested, by the enemy, by paying a small fine or by hiring substitutes for their drafted or personal military duties. The District of Hackensack became the separating lines between the contending parties during the war, we were repeatedly plundered, and left destitute of any other bed to lay upon, except that of straw: on several occasions, the clothes were torn from our backs, and the bread and the means of purchasing it were taken from us.

In the year 1777, my brother, Elias Romaine, obtained a captaincy in the Jersey line and was stationed by Colonel [Theunis] Dey, the commander of the regiment, at the nearest outpost, the Liberty Pole, in Bergen County. Being advised by my father and brother to enlist, as all prospect and means of completing my education were lost by the war, I did accordingly enlist, in the fall of the same year, at the age of fifteen years and three months, or thereabouts, in my said brother's company of militia and was accepted as a sergeant thereof, in which station I became very useful; the education, which I had received in this city, before our family fled from it, enabled me to perform successfully the various duties of the company and regiment, in making out orders, pay rolls etc. In this my first enlistment in 1777 I served not less than three months.

In the spring of the year 1778, I was enrolled in the year's service, under my said brother, Captain Elias Romaine, in the same regiment, of Colonel Dey, at the Liberty Pole, during which service he was frequently ordered to various posts, under other officers during that year, and also under officers of the standing troops. Under Captain John Outwater, at Hackensack town, he served not less than three months. Under Captain Samuel Demarest, at New Bridge, & under Captain *[Joshua]* Bowman, of the Standing troops, for a short time. Under Captain John Vreeland, at Polifly, not less than two months. Under Captain *[Peter]* Ward at Acquackanonk, not less than one month, and the remainder of the year, under my brother Captain Romaine. In the course of my terms I became twice a guide to General *[Anthony]* Wayne, when his head quarters were at Acquackanonk, in his excursions upon the lines. I was also in the reserve line of militia when Paulus Hook was stormed by Major *[Henry]* Lee and the garrison force of the enemy made prisoners of war. I was also in the unsuccessful attack on the blockhouse in Bergen Woods, near the margin of the Hudson River, when our troops were led by General Wayne. I was also at the side of Sergeant *[Silvester]* Marius, in a severe conflict upon the lines. I was also engaged throughout the whole day, when the enemy burned Paramus and Hoppertown, about eight miles above New Bridge. The troops harassed the rear and flanks of the enemy, in their march to the Hoppers Mills, and continued to do so, in their final retreat back to Fort Lee; at which place they re-crossed the Hudson for Fort Washington, their stronghold during the war, we recaptured almost all the baggage and effects which they had plundered. In the course of the conflict the enemy horse made three attempts of attack, on our several companies, pressing on their flanks and rear, but at no time did they come to a charge. On one occasion, however, where I was present, they surprised about one hundred of us, in a clear field: they advanced at full speed and with apparent determination: we instantly formed, as retreat was useless, when the enemy declined the attack and filed off. Our officers, notwithstanding to the great mortification, forbid us to fire, though the enemy was at easy distance shot. I was also in a very severe affair of arms, at the Liberty Pole, where my brother was in command, against the sudden attack of a far

Benjamin Romaine recounts in great detail his company's engagements with the British force on its return from Hoppertown on April 16, 1780. The house of John Hopper, the scene of the greatest action during the fight, was burned in an effort to compel the defenders to surrender. The building housing this fine restaurant in modern Ho-Ho-Kus was built soon afterward on what is most likely the remains of the Hopper House. *Courtesy of Todd W. Braisted.*

superior number of British horse: we there lost a considerable number of our company in killed, wounded and prisoners: the enemy were severely handled at the point of the woods at which we arrived entering the clear field where the conflict began. I was also under the personal command of Colonel Dey when the whole County of Bergen was summoned to dislodge the enemy from Fort Lee, where they had commenced the re-establishment of an outpost. The attack was made at daybreak and the enemy fled in great precipitation, and never again attempted to form a station at that place.

My next service was under Captain John Huyler, at Closter, in the same regiment of Colonel Dey having been drafted to perform the same; in which service I continued not less than three months: the service was rendered in the spring of 1779 or 1780.

My next service was under Captain Thomas Blanch, at Closter, in the same regiment, under whom I served for a period not less than two months: during this service, I was engaged with the enemy, at the burning of Closter, and also at the subsequent burning of Schraalenburgh, where my mother and myself, after my father's death, resided. Being drafted, I entered this service in the fall of 1779 or 1780.

On the 6th day of September 1781, myself with five others, while in arms at Closter, was taken by surprise of the enemy, who was led to the place of our nightly seclusion, to which we were accustomed to retire, when off of duty, not daring to sleep in our houses. This place of seclusion was in the thick woods, and near it were driven our horses and cattle for safety. They were led to it by one Samuel Cole, who perpetrated this act of treachery: he was of Closter, a Tory resident of our neighborhood. He led on the enemy in his own person, we were made prisoners, though not then in actual enlistment, and with our horses and cattle were hastened down to this City, where we were put in prison and held for seven weeks. Our exchange was effected nearly the exact time Cornwallis was taken, we returned to our homes, and I entered on military duty in my company beat as theretofore and continued therein till the end of the war. At our capture, one Elias Day was pierced through the thigh with a bayonet, and myself was slightly wounded in the arm with a like weapon, by Captain William Harding the chief of the gang; who saith, it was only his intention to make me feel a little for abusing Sam Cole, their guide.

Some time thereafter, in the latter part of 1781 or beginning of 1782, I entered the company beat of Captain James Christie, at Schraalenburgh in the same regiment, under whom I served for a period not less than three months. I was then voted an ensign of the company beat and performed the duty during the whole remainder of the war. It was then declared that my commission was come on, but had been misplaced: this was deemed, at the time, a matter of little consequence, as the commissions of several of the officers were lost. I performed the duty of ensign in the company beat to the end of the war and full three months of active and enrolled volunteer duty.

The number of affairs of arms to which I was engaged was about twenty seven, exclusive of slight skirmishes, and encounters, which were of frequent occurrences sometimes daily when the opposite scouting parties met.

I recapitulate to the best of my knowledge and belief, for it is not now possible after a lapse of more than fifty years and when young and heedless, to recollect the months or even the years in which services were performed with sufficient accuracy for <u>positive affidavits</u> and state that me first enlistment was in my brother's company stationed at the Liberty Pole in the fall of 1777, as a sergeant, and served three or four months, say 3 *[months]*

In 1778 I was enrolled in the year volunteer service, under my said brother, also at the Liberty Pole and as sergeant, and during that year, was ordered on duty to other posts viz. Capt. John

Outwater in Hackensack town	3 *[months]*	
Under Captain Demarest at New Bridge	3 *[months]*	
Under Captain Vreeland at Polifly	2 *[months]*	
Under Captain Bowman, of the Standing troops, by order of my brother and on Captain Bowman's request	1 *[month]*	
Under Captain Ward at Acquackanonk	1 *[month]*	
Under my brother to complete the year's service	<u>2</u> *[months]*	
[Total]	1 *[year]* 3 *[months]*	

In 1781, a prisoner of war seven weeks…

These services exclusive of all those personal turnouts on every alarm and actual eruption of the enemy which were of daily and nightly apprehension and of frequent execution during the whole war when off regular enlistment and at home, on company service, it became my duty to warn every person in the beat to turn out, this was indispensable to secure the fines on those who refused personal service. To estimate the time of service in these cases would swell the amount far beyond the above recapitulated duties. On one of these warning performances, my retreat was cut off at the Old Bridge Creek, about eighty feet wide when I crossed on the back of my horse. The canoe there was locked and the key refused to me by the old Tory who owned it. In truth and in fact, the Whigs in this district of country, may be truly said to have been soldiers during the whole of the Revolutionary War. I never received a written discharge from the services: that being then very little heeded, nor did I ever receive a written commission. I have no documentary evidence. All my officers to the best of my knowledge and belief are now dead: except Captain Samuel Demarest, who resides somewhere in the western part of the state, and whose testimony could be procured only with great difficulty: but Silvester Marius, James Riker and Samuel Vervalen, fellow soldiers, can testify to my services. The Reverend John Demarest and John Hopson can testify to my character for veracity and their belief of my services as a soldier of the Revolution. I hereby relinquish every claim whatever to a pension or annuity except the present and declare that my name is not on the pension roll of any agency of any state.

Romaine's initial submittal was rejected and further information required, an extract of which appears here:

On my way home, this <u>fifteen months</u> of time, only awarded to me for services to my country during the Revolutionary War, became extremely afflicting, from the manifest injustice I had done to my past history of facts, and more to the honor of a large and rising family, who had been led to understand my services far more than fifteen months; and also to the oaths of my contemporaries addressed in my presentment.

It was not the annual pittance I was to receive during the remnant of "<u>life</u>" (this I need not) but it was the "<u>record</u>" of the time, and the manner in which it now stands <u>recorded</u>, which gives to me the most poignant affliction; when to my positive knowledge, I had performed more than three years of actual military duty, "<u>both in the field and Garrison</u>," during the revolutionary struggle, and these exclusive of other contingencies of affective service.

I was always ardent in obedience to orders in the performance of military duty; nor do I believe that a single man <u>now lives</u> who has passed more peril in life, in arms, and by wounds and <u>imprisonment</u> than myself, during the Revolutionary War; and which, the minor parts of a true history of those times, in my local position on the lines, may require of me some future development.

If my presentment be defective and inadmissible in its details according to the strict letter of the law in this case, I must lament the lapse of time, and an imperfect recollection myself, and more especially the failure, as would seem, in technical arrangement, about which I know little, to make it better understood, and suited to existing regulations. It was written <u>in my own way</u> and put in the present order of arrangement, by a loop, fixed by my grandson Dillon and is now in your bureau subject to all its merits and deficiencies.

I still have it in my power to transmit to you, if required, many further witnesses in the case. I had, as advised, only sought barely sufficient time in my declaration to make out the two years as required by the Treasury regulations.

The disallowance of my seven weeks imprisonment, when every thing but death had been suffered, and me a wounded prisoner, appears to my mind to have become legalized by my regular exchange, though "not in actual service when taken." You will remember my telling you that, at the time of my capture, I had only been discharged, and returned home, one or two days from a regular months tour of duty.

From that which passed in your office, I must here sketch my three or four (I now know it to have been four) months service under my brother, at the command of my father in 1777. I had pleaded excuse from going to school, as my father had requested, (we then lived on the lines where both the belligerent parties had alternate possession.) One evening my father came into the house with a large English musket, and its appendages, with a cartouch box filled with 24 rounds of ball cartridges. He sat the musket in the closet; mother asked his meaning, he answered not. In the early morning he bid me rise, and buckled on me the armor, and said, "you have refused to make effort with me to perfect your education, now go to your brother and defend your country!" These trying moments, sir, to the family, can never cease to be appreciated, while a particle of life remains, and the effect of this command has never ceased to influence my life and conduct (now in protected strain) and "in defense of my country;" and very specially in support of its present united Constitution of general government, and opposed to that venal tendency of state sovereignty aberrations, as under the old Confederation, by whomsoever or in whatever form these may make appearance, as heretofore, through influential and disappointed state individuals. These I shall never cease to oppose by every talent, and every remaining energy of my life. Such are the main Germes, the Bohun Upas, or tree of death to our happy Union.

To resume. I proceeded to the Liberty Pole to my brother's quarters, was gazed upon through the range of Tory neighborhood, it was exclaimed, that old Rebel has now also sent his youngest son to join his other son, at the Liberty Pole, etc.

My father was subsequently plundered of every useful article. The little furniture dashed to pieces, and not a second shirt was left us, as stated in my declaration.

For this my said first month of substitute duty I received eight dollars bounty, and gave it to my mother. I now grieve to state that, this said first month, and the subsequent three, "would be judged of by you, as of doubtful character," as to the present enumeration of time to be allowed to me in the present case; if any deduction or alteration be made from the present decision or any other decision, I hope, sir, that, if every other part of my presentment be found discrepant, or erroneous, that first three or four

Implements of war in the county, including a tin cartridge box found on a farm in Bergenfield, a bullet mold and two musket balls, one of which had impacted against the walls of the Zabriskie-Steuben House at New Bridge during one of the skirmishes there. *Courtesy of the Bergen County Historical Society.*

months of time, may be deemed legitimate, nevertheless my "<u>minority</u>," as was observed.

It will be seen in my first declaration, that a small portion only of my year services in 1778, and a part of 1779, were performed under my brother, though first enrolled under him. I therefore endeavored to state, in the most accurate way I was able, the names of the officers, and the times of my service under each of them that year. My statement you will find in a great degree, to correspond with the testimony of my witnesses, all made distinct and apart from each other.

At one time it was deemed that one out-post required more defensive force than another, and those years men were selected and detailed, also from other companies, to such changing and varied duties. They were also constantly sought for as guides and recruiting service, to the standing troops, and also to direct the officers and men from the back-woods militia on their tours of duty on the lines. They were also drill-men to the militia. I have detailed a few instances in regard to myself in my first declaration.

The fact truly is, that these years men formed "a kind of flying camp during the war" as described to you in a joint letter of Lewis and Silas Condict, and Theo' Frelinghuysen, who says "that my father was the captain of an artillery company raised for one year." We were repeatedly ordered to various commands, and to every point of most imminent danger.

When the present law of pension was formed, it is clear to my mind, that justice demanded on a due comparison of services, dangers and distresses, of the immediate inhabitants, who remained on the lines, and true to their country, that, when captured, and whether on actual duty or not, ought instantly to have been considered, and rewarded as if in actual enlistment, and especially so, as such citizens were deprived of all usefulness to their destitute families; instead of this the small remnant of these men are now abandoned to this their fate, and are actually disfranchised in the common benefit of Pension!!! These inhabitants were the most effective guards, and defense to the back neighborhoods, not only, but to the interior of the whole state of New Jersey and elsewhere. Would these men be now disfranchised on a review of this weighty important point of a just retribution for national attachment. When on oath, not to take arms against his majesty (as their liberation was repeatedly tendered) thousands have died rather than take such oath!

The above not having the desired effect, Romaine appealed one last time to the Secretary of War:

New York 30th January 1835.
[To] The honorable
Lewis Cass Secretary
of War Washington
City very Specially

Sir,

I perceive that the pension law is about to be amended. I have made two presentments of my claims, written in plain current detail, the latter explanatory of the first, both appear mostly wanting of accuracy in the dates of service; as by the printed rules, sent to me by Mr. Edwards, together with the last letter, of date 11th August last, requesting "further explanation," and which yet remains unanswered by me, in expectation of more satisfactory detail.

Before I proceed, permit me, Sir, to state to you, and the gentlemen of the pension department, to re-examine my remarks contained in both my presentments, and specially that which is explanatory of the first, respecting certain citizens who continued to dwell on the lines, in New Jersey, with their families, and who performed every duty of arms during the Revolutionary War always at the great peril of life, liberty, and property; and who remain excluded from their country's bounty, however their long confinement and sufferings may have been, if made prisoners when not happening to be "in actual enlistment." On you, Sir, much will depend to afford such citizens who yet linger among us, a just and most merited relief.

I have given my aid, and best recollections to many fellow soldiers, and on all occasions the greatest difficulties occur in the knowledge of the years and months of service, with sufficient accuracy for positive affidavits. I find in both my presentments, "the rank and names of officers," "each term of engagement," "the particular place and places of service" "the amount of time served," are far better remembered, at this late day, and I am surprised to find, in both my presentments, so accurate conformity with the printed requisitions, in these respects, both in my own recollections and those of my witnesses.

Mr. Edwards says in his said letter, "that the omission of dates in the original and "supplemental declarations, renders it difficult to ascertain whether some of the terms "asserted in the one may not be included in the more general items of the other." These remarks are strictly correct, and stand self evident in the several and distinct affidavits of my witnesses, each declaring, more or less, to the same facts. To separate these blendings of the same time, to a true conformity with the solemnity of my declarations, has given to me great concern and much reflection; though I had no idea of want of time to secure to me, the full benefit of the law of 7th June 1832.

Mr. Edwards requests me to state "more particularly, the period term, and grade of each tour." I can only say here, that, on my first enlistment I obtained the grade of sergeant, and do not recollect that at any subsequent service, whether by regular draft duty, substitute or volunteer. That the grade of Sergeant was omitted to be conferred on me, (except the time I served as ensign under Captain Christie.) I will state here that my knowledge of discipline acquired by an almost continued service from very early life, rendered such grade efficient in any corps or company to which I became attached.

Mr. Edwards in his said last letter also says "In the original declaration you allege that "you entered the <u>year service</u>, and served several terms under different officers, and the "remainder of the year under your brother, this requires some explanation." I trust, Sir, that on a re-examination of my papers, a full account of these "<u>several terms</u>" throughout that year, and the reasons there given, will be found satisfactorily stated, and performed in regular and connected course.

If I understand Mr. Edwards, he requests also to know the <u>grade</u> and names of the person or persons for whom I served as substitute, of this I have no knowledge specially; the officers provided the substitute, and paid him the bounty obtained. There were certain militia officers opposed to the war, who regularly paid substitute bounty, rather than incur the fines.

If, sir, when commanded to warn out the dissaffected by the "<u>militia</u>" officers, of my regular company beat, on all occasions of real or apprehended approach of the enemy, to fix the fines on them—if these orders be of the "<u>competent authority</u>," mentioned in the printed regulations, then my "<u>terms</u>," "<u>tours</u>," and detentions, for days and weeks together;—as orderly sergeant, swell my amount of time served, to months beyond the present estimate.

I will relate one of those warning "<u>tours</u>." My retreat was cut off at the Old Bridge Creek (a few miles above Hackensack) about eighty feet wide, and deep water. The canoe was locked, and the key refused to me by the old Tory owner; and when I had crossed, on the back of my little fox horse, was, shortly after fired upon several times, and until out of reach; whether by the disaffected residents, or the enemy in regular arms I know not. A Sergeant <u>Samuel Banta</u>, was severely wounded, and several others fired upon in the performance of like duties…

CHAPTER 16

GEORGE G. RYERSON

Pompton

*T*he Ryerson family, predominant in the northwestern part of the county, extending toward Morris, was very active on both sides of the conflict, providing both officers and enlisted men, with four serving in the Bergen County Militia and five in the New Jersey Volunteers. Samuel Ryerson would make his military name serving under the noted Patrick Ferguson at King's Mountain in South Carolina, having his ring finger shot off during the battle, while the object of this chapter, George G. Ryerson, took part in the January 1780 attack on the Loyalist Ryerson's battalion in his absence.

It is this latter action that is of interest, being one of the rare times some of the county's militia took the offensive on British held ground. Staten Island had been the initial place of British debarkation in early July 1776 and in 1780 was still a major part of their defenses for New York City. It was also the garrison home for Abraham Van Buskirk and his New Jersey Volunteers, occupying the ferry house and grounds of Isaac Decker, a captain in the island's Loyalist militia. Decker's Ferry, opposite Bergen Point, was the principal outpost of the northern part of the island, its main forts situated at Richmond in the center and the Flagstaff and Watering Place in the east.

The winter of 1779–1780 was the coldest in known memory at the time. The islands of New York ceased to be such, with the rivers, kills and harbor frozen over. Staten Island, garrisoned by one British, one Hessian and four Provincial battalions, mustered about two thousand men for its defense. Seizing on the opportunity to give the British a bloody nose, if not more, General Washington authorized an expedition of about three thousand infantry, cavalry and artillery, commanded by Major General William Alexander, a.k.a. Lord Stirling, to cross over the ice early in the morning of January 15 and surprise the British before they could take to their forts. The surprise failed. Loyalist spies in New Jersey *had advance warning and gave notice to the British. Abraham Van Buskirk and his men retreated to the forts on the east end, while the other corps occupied their fortifications and prepared for a possible siege. The severity of the weather would never have permitted such a thing, though. Lieutenant Colonel John Graves Simcoe of the Queen's American Rangers, stationed in a fort at Richmond, described his view of the Continental Army's advance:*

> While the troops in the enemy's front, on their arrival at the heights opposite to the British redoubts, halted for the rear to close up, they were permitted to make fires, which increased the power of the frost, and rendered them totally unable to proceed, and the severity of the night affecting the whole of them, many lost their limbs, and several their lives. There were vast mounds of snow drifted before the redoubts, which Lord Stirling gave as his reason for not attempting them...

Simcoe also revealed that if his fort had been stormed, his men had prepared a nasty surprise for the attackers, spike nails driven through boards and placed upwards, concealed in the snow leading to his post.

It was during the withdrawal that George G. Ryerson was wounded. As British commanding officer Brigadier General Thomas Stirling wrote:

> ...the enemy were discovered going off by Decker's Ferry, a party of 200 men were ordered immediately to follow them and 20 Light Dragoons; Lieutenant [William] Stewart of the Provincial Light Horse who commanded them and Cornet Tucker of the 17th [Light Dragoons] made a gallant charge on their rear and took a sergeant and four men prisoners, but our foot not being able to keep pace with them, nothing more could be done...

The composition of the militia in which Ryerson was a part is not exactly known, other than that men from Bergen, Essex and Morris were a part of it. Likewise, their actual role in the invasion is unclear, as Washington made no mention of any in his extensive instructions to Lord Stirling. Also in violation of Washington's direct orders against plundering, both Continentals and militia took advantage of the situation. As the Reverend Charles Inglis recorded in his journal: "The Rebels plundered all the loyal inhabitants, carrying off all movables, & stripping even old women, sick persons & children."

The main weapon of any cavalryman at the time of the American Revolution was the sword. Lieutenant Ryerson would have seen weapons such as this in the hands of the cavalry pursuing his troops on their retreat off Staten Island. *Courtesy of the Bergen County Historical Society.*

Sixteen months after his ordeal on Staten Island, Lieutenant Ryerson was engaged against Loyalists once again, this time Thomas Ward's Refugees at Fort Lee. During the period of May 14–18, there were three distinct engagements between the Refugees and the militia, in each of which the latter was defeated. After attempts at fortifying during the day, Ward's men would spend the night in relative safety on board their shipping in the Hudson. This led to the last of the three engagements and the one that Ryerson in particular took part, as described in the May 19 edition of the Royal Gazette:

> This morning, just after sun-rise, as they were proceeding in order to continue the work they had begun to erect, the advanced party, consisting of about ten men, had nearly got within the works, when they perceived them to be in the possession of the enemy, who made two of the party prisoners; the rest gave their fire, and ran off down the hill; the rebels pursuing, Captain Harding ordered a field piece to be placed in such a position which, with the fire from a gun boat, and the musketry, obliged them to return up the hill. Captain Harding advanced through a valley that led up the hill, and gained the right flank of the enemy, whom he instantly charged, and obliged to quit the works they were in possession of, retreating in great confusion, and leaving behind them 1 man killed and 1 wounded; they also took off with them several who were badly wounded; Captain Harding pursued the enemy to the heights of the English Neighborhood, but was not able to come up with them; the Refugees have only had one man slightly wounded, and two captured. The rebel party consisted of militia and one years men, and amounted to upwards of four hundred men.

Ryerson's pension application is No. S1098.

On this *[blank]* day of July 1833, personally appeared before the subscriber a justice of the peace in and for the County *[of Bergen]* and State *[of New Jersey]* George G. Ryerson of Pompton in said county aged 79 years and personally well known in said county and to the subscriber as a man of truth and good standing and being duly sworn saith that he is the same George G. Ryerson who on the 31st day of October 1832 made a declaration under oath of his revolutionary services in order to obtain the benefit of the Act of Congress passed June 7th 1832 which was done in open court then sitting in and for the county of *[Bergen]* aforesaid; when his original serving declaration was made out, the pressure of business before the court was such as to prevent him from detailing minutely each tour of duty he performed and specifying as accurately as he has since learned was necessary, the officers who commanded on such occasion and the time and nature of the duty—he has endeavored to refresh his memory by bestowing more thought and reflection on the subject and desires that the Secretary of War and Commissioner of Pensions will receive this as his amended declaration, in which he will endeavor to set forth more specifically and in as much detail as possible his memory will allow, of the revolutionary services he performed.

He served two months, in the fall of 1776 as a volunteer in a company of horse under Captain Nicholas Jones, was marched from Pompton, Bergen County to Elizabeth Town, Essex County where he was stationed, doing vidette duty between the two counties. Colonel Theunis Dey commanded the regiment of which this company was a part—though we were not under his immediate command. Served the time, was discharged and went home.

Having received a commission as lieutenant from the then governor of the State of New Jersey and signed by him William Livingston, the date of which he cannot recollect, as it is lost but knows it was in the year 1777 when he acted in all his tours throughout the war in capacity of lieutenant.

He served one month in the winter of 1776 & 1777 under Captain *[Peter]* Ward as lieutenant. Was marched from Pompton, Bergen County to Short Hills and Metuchen near New Brunswick, thence to Elizabeth Town, Newark and Belleville, thinks the British were at New Brunswick at the same time; having served the time was discharged at Belleville. This duty was as volunteer, Colonel Theunis Dey commanding regiment.

He served one month, in the spring of 1777 under Captain Peter Ward as lieutenant and volunteer, was marched from Pompton to Hoppers Mill, County of Bergen, the British then lying at the English Neighborhood, four miles from Hoppers Mill at the same time. Captain Ward being absent had the charge of the company at this time, doing guard duty. Served the time and was discharged, Colonel Dey commanding regiment.

He served two months in the winter of 1780 as a lieutenant having volunteered under Captain John Mead, stationed at Elizabeth Town, Essex County, having marched from Pompton in Bergen County; during this service he was of a party of about eighteen hundred volunteers, who crossed on the ice and attacked the British on Staten Island, at which time they succeeded in driving and pursuing the enemy to a place now called quarantine ground.

That the Americans lay near the heights of that place, through the course of the succeeding night, was attacked by the British early next morning and obliged to retreat. That in this engagement he received a wound from the enemy, a musket ball passed through his right leg, in consequence of which, he was conveyed back to Elizabeth Town, where he was confined for several weeks, and then returned home. Through the error of the drawer this tour is not in order of time* He served two months in spring of 1778, as lieutenant, having been balloted under Captain John Mead, stationed at Hackensack, guarding prisoners confined in jail of said place, and that at the same time, two of the prisoners were executed. Served the time and was discharged, Colonel Theunis Dey commanding regiment.

He served two months in June, July and August in the year of 1778 as a lieutenant having volunteered, under Captain Peter Ward, was stationed at Bergen Point, Hackensack and other places in Bergen County doing duty as guard and other services as required. Served the time and was discharged, Colonel Theunis Dey commanding regiment.

He served one month in the fall of 1778 as lieutenant being balloted, under Captain Peter Ward, Colonel Dey commanding, was stationed at Paramus doing guard duty, protecting the inhabitants from the depredations of the enemy British, Refugees and Tories. Served the time and was discharged.

He served one month in the spring, 1779 as he believes, as lieutenant being balloted, under Captain John Mead, was stationed at Paramus, Bergen County during which the company was frequently divided into squads of twenty to thirty men each, whose duty was to scour the county and intercept the gangs of Refugees, horse thieves and plundering parties, that they were in the habit of distressing the inhabitants and aiding the enemy. Colonel Theunis Dey commanding regiment. Served the time and was discharged.

He served two months in the months of June, July & August in the year of 1779, being balloted under Captain Peter Ward as lieutenant. Captain Ward being absent, had the command for some time. Was stationed at Hackensack, Bergen County and Newark, Essex County under the command of Colonel [*Captain*] John N. Cumming. That on this occasion they kept up a chain of sentinels from Newark to Hackensack with orders to intercept all deserters or other citizens travelling in the direction of the City of New York. Served the time and was discharged.

He served 6 weeks in October and November of the year 1779 as lieutenant being balloted under Captain Peter Ward, Colonel Theunis Dey commanding regiment, stationed at Pompton, Bergen County having received the command of about thirty men having orders to march from place to place watching the movements of the enemy, frequently intercepting their marauding parties and retaking horses, cattle and other plunder from them. General *[Nathaniel]* Heard had command of the brigade on this occasion, served the time and was discharged.

He served one month in the spring of 1780 as lieutenant having volunteered under Captain John Mead, was stationed at Pompton, doing guard duty and other services as mentioned in other tours. Colonel Theunis Dey commanding. Served the time and was discharged.

He served one month believes in May and June of 1780 as lieutenant being balloted under Captain Henry Van Bryck, was stationed at Hackensack. While on this station the British and Refugees, succeeded in burning and destroying the Court House of Hackensack and the dwelling house of Adam Boyd. Colonel Dey commanding regiment. Served the time and was discharged.

He served one month, thinks it was in the spring of 1781, and was not mentioned in his declaration, under Captain Board as lieutenant and volunteered, was stationed at Hackensack, doing guard duty and other services as was required. Colonel Dey commanding regiment and *[John]* Mauritius Goetschius Major—served the time and was discharged.

His last tour that he can remember, as to nature and time was in the summer of 1782 *[1781]* under Captain Peter Ward as lieutenant and volunteer. Was stationed at English Neighborhood, Bergen County, during which service he was in command of the company, in absence of Captain Ward and was with a party that surprised and recaptured Fort Lee from the British and Refugees. That a Captain Leonard of the regular army had the command of the detachment on this occasion—a British Lieutenant *[James]* Hamilton was among the prisoners taken at that time. Colonel Theunis Dey commanding the militia, stationed at the English Neighborhood. This service was for two months. Having served the time was verbally discharged at Hackensack, Bergen County, in which county all his services where rendered, if not they are particularly mentioned.

From the great length of time which has elapsed since the before recited services were rendered many particulars must have escaped his memory. He has stated all which he can remember, as connected with his services, and which are calculated to explain them. In the order of time and in the names perhaps of some of his superior officers, he may in some instances perhaps have fallen into mistakes. He asks a reasonable allowance for the frailty of human memory; whilst he has faithfully endeavored to adhere conscientiously to the truth, in all the events and occurrences of which he has spoken. And he verily believes that he faithfully served his country in the War of the Revolution for the full period of twenty and a half months. Two months as a Private and eighteen & a half as lieutenant—for which term of months he claims a pension from the United States under the Act of Congress of June 7th 1832.

Sworn and Subscribed
to before me this *[blank]* day of *[blank]*

*Before subscribing the applicant discovered that there was an error in the time of the two months service under Captain Mead it being in this declaration in order of 1778, and on further consideration, thinks General Dickinson was not there on that Occasion but knows Lord Stirling was.

CHAPTER 17

PETER VAN ALLEN

Franklin Township

*T*he Van Allen family was another prominent Bergen County family divided by the war. Representing the Whig side we have Peter Van Allen, a native of Franklin Township, and one of the older pensioners. Van Allen served for the entire war, from the construction of Fort Lee in 1776 through the battle there five years later, where his cousin Ensign John Van Allen was wounded in action against the Refugees. Among the key incidents in Van Allen's career was the killing of John Berry, a Hackensack Loyalist serving under Thomas Ward. Known as "John the Regular" to the Whigs, presumably for some previous service in the British Army, Berry was active in collecting intelligence in the county the previous winter and was considered a great risk to the militia. Happy indeed then was Governor William Livingston when he received word on May 26, 1780, from Captains Thomas Blanch and John Huyler on the success of their expedition to Bergen Neck with a hefty force of fifty militia: "Having arranged our Detachment in such manner, as to intercept any Parties of the Enemy which might be out we again began our march, and to our great satisfaction soon fell in with a Party of six men of whom two were killed and two taken Prisoner. Amongst the former was the noted Murderer & Thief John Berry alias John the Regular who behaved in every respect like a man stimulated by despair…" Van Allen was not the only militiaman who would proudly take credit for being of that party. It is not known what Van Allen is referencing about the "Hessian picket" (or guard) at Paramus. However, given that he mentioned it directly after his reference to Aaron Burr, it is most likely he is speaking of the surprise of the British picket at Robert Timpany's schoolhouse near New Bridge during the 1777 British Grand Forage, as discussed previously by David Ritzema Bogert. Van Allen's pension application is registered as No. S6301.

The life of the militia and state troops, such as this reenactor from Outwater's Company, was often one of boredom, punctuated by patrols and the occasional brush with the enemy. Lacking uniforms, they served in the clothes they lived in every day. *Courtesy of Todd W. Braisted.*

On this 31 day of October 1832, personally appeared in open court, before the judges of the Inferior Court of Common Pleas in and for the County of Bergen now sitting, Peter Van Allen a resident of Saddle River in the County of Bergen and State of New Jersey, aged eighty four years, who being first duly sworn according to law, doth on his oath make the following declaration, in order to obtain the benefit of the Act of Congress, passed June 7, 1832.

That he entered the service of the United States under the following named officers, and served as herein stated. That he was born in that part of the County of Bergen now called Franklin on the 15th day of September 1748, according to the traditional account of his age, the record of which, having been lost or destroyed. That he resided at the place now called Franklin, at the commencement of the Revolutionary War and enlisted as a volunteer in a company commanded by Captain Joseph Board for three months, and in the summer of 1776 was marched to the City of New York and immediately after the battle on Long Island was marched to Bergen Point and there stationed as a guard; a portion of the British Army was lying on Staten Island, during the same time. That he served out the period of his enlistment. That he volunteered and performed three months service under Captain [Jost] Beam. That he thinks that a portion of the service under Captain Beam was employed in building Fort Lee on the Hudson River and was stationed a part of the time at the English Neighborhood. That he performed several monthly tours of service under Captain [Crynes] Bartholf. That he enlisted and performed three months service under Captain [Peter] Fell who commanded the company called the Rangers, John Van Allen was a lieutenant of the same company. Aaron Burr, was in commission and in some way attached to the same corps, but cannot tell what rank he bore at the time; he may have only had the command, as a field officer, on one occasion. That he recollects of his being with the company when they succeeded in taking the Hessian picket guard near Paramus. That he performed three months service under Captain Thomas Blanch. Thinks he was stationed at Hackensack during that time. That he performed three months service under Captain [John] Outwater. That he performed three months service, per enlistment, under Captain Joseph Board at which time the company was stationed at Mill Stone. Col. Theunis Dey commanded the regiment. The British was lying at New Brunswick at the same time. That he was enlisted and performed three months service under Captain Uriah Ryerson. The only field officers he can now recollect under whom he served are Colonel Dey and Major [John Mauritius] Goetschius. That he was in the service of

The Wortendyke Barn in Park Ridge is typical of Bergen's large Dutch outbuildings of the time. Today it is a museum, operated by the county. *Courtesy of Bergen County Division of Cultural and History Affairs.*

the United States during the Revolutionary War from the commencement, to the end thereof, in all not less than three years, but cannot, at this time recollect the names of any of the officers other than above mentioned. That he was in an engagement with the British near Paramus and at Hoppers Mills. That he was in an engagement with the British *[and]* Refugees near Hackensack. Thinks General *[William]* Winds commanded, and after the battle he retreated on to a hill near Slotterdam, and lay through the night, during a violent storm, and without shelter. That he was once engaged with the Refugees at a place called the little ferry on the Hackensack River. That he was one of a party and assisted in taking John Berry a Refugee Regular who had been advertised as an outlaw on account of the repeated murders & outrages committed. That on account of the many infirmities under which he is laboring it is impossible to give a more detailed account of the times, places, or circumstances, than is above stated. That he now recollects of being in an engagement with the British & Refugees at Fort Lee on the Hudson River and at which time his cousin John Van Allen, a member of the same company, was wounded. That he saw many of the officers of the

Regular army during his said service but cannot now recollect them by name. General Washington quartered at his house on one occasion about a week; his recollection is very indistinct as to any of the field officers with whom he served. That at the close of the war he returned to his native place and since which he has continued to reside. That he has no documentary evidence; he has no recollection of ever receiving a written or printed discharge. That he knows of no other persons whose testimony he can produce who can testify to his service…

He hereby relinquishes every claim whatever to a pension or annuity except the present, and declares that his name is not on the Pension Roll of the Agency of any of the United States.

CHAPTER 18

WILLIAM VAN ALLEN

Hackensack Township

*O*n the opposite end of the political spectrum from Peter Van Allen was Captain William Van Allen of Hackensack Township. While sparse on information concerning his services during the war, Van Allen's claim has the advantage of showing his actual property and monetary losses because of the conflict. Van Allen was the senior captain in Abraham Van Buskirk's Fourth Battalion, New Jersey Volunteers, with his commission bearing the date of November 23, 1776. Van Allen was credited with taking the very first prisoners by the battalion, when on December 6, 1776, the corps left New Bridge and patrolled to the northward, as described by the New-York Gazette and the Weekly Mercury: *"The New–Jersey Volunteers hearing, that a Party of Rebel Officers were lodged at a little Distance from Tappan, immediately set out in Quest of them, and took one Rebel Captain, and two Lieutenants, Prisoners."* The Loyalist also claims to have hidden William Bayard in 1776. Bayard was a very wealthy resident of both Bergen County and across the border in Orange County, New York, where he was colonel of the militia. His residence in Bergen County was in Hoboken, known at the time as "Hoebuck" and which was used as a garrison post by Van Allen and the rest of the battalion for several months in 1779. Van Allen lived on the east side of the Hackensack River, at New Bridge, and was undoubtedly well acquainted with Abraham Van Buskirk. This no doubt contributed to his obtaining a commission so quickly, as well as his raising dozens of men to serve in his company. Van Allen was proscribed and banished for high treason. His house, described as a one-story stone dwelling, "well situated," was purchased by Cornelius Hogeland. William had purchased the house from John Earl just five days before hostilities commenced at Lexington and Concord in 1775. Van Allen settled along with many families of the battalion in Sunbury County,

Officers provided their own uniforms, weapons and camp equipage, often including luxuries unknown to common soldiers. This brazier served the function of a personal cooking station for an officer or gentleman, easily accommodating a teapot or similarly sized vessel. *Courtesy of the Bergen County Historical Society.*

New Brunswick, after the war. His son Henry, commissioned an ensign in 1781, settled in York County of the same province.

That your memorialist on account of his loyalty to His Majesty & attachment to the British Government was obliged to quit his habitation & estate in Hackensack Precinct, New Jersey & take refuge within the lines at New York in November 1776.

That your memorialist was so fortunate as to protect and convey safely within the lines Colonel William Bayard at a time when the Rebels offered a reward for him of £500.

That your memorialist raised at his own expense a full company of men & served as a captain during the war & in the year 1783 came with his regiment to Nova Scotia.

That the Rebels have seized & confiscated a Freehold Estate belonging to your memorialist in Hackensack Precinct aforesaid consisting of one lot of land with a house, barn & outhouses valued by your memorialist at not less than £500 New York Currency & on which there was no mortgage.

That your memorialist also lost as follows

Household furniture	14.	16	0.
One ton hay	4.	0.	0.
One ox	5.	0.	0.
Lawful paper money	33.	6.	9.
Debt due from Anthony Skeler	30.	14.	1.
Ditto from Abraham Blauvelt	4.	0.	0.
Book Debts supposed good	82.	18.	0.
14 Bushels Indian Corn	2.	9.	0.
New York Currency	£177.	3.	10.

All which your memorialist humbly submits in full confidence that such recompense & compensation shall be made him as to equity & justice shall appertain.

CHAPTER 19

GEORGE VAN BUSKIRK

Closter

George Van Buskirk was among the relative handful of county residents who volunteered for service in the Continental army at the beginning of the war. Enlisting in 1776 for one year in the Third New Jersey Battalion, he took part with his corps in the Northern Campaign, away from the main theater of operations around New York City. Traveling up the Hudson to Albany, the corps moved west to Johnson Hall, the manor house of the Mohawk Valley's most influential Loyalist, Sir John Johnson. Johnson, learning he was to be arrested by the troops, fled to Canada with about 170 of his tenants. The New Jerseyians, commanded by Colonel Elias Dayton, placed a very pregnant Lady Johnson under arrest, sending her to Albany to be held as a hostage, then took to plundering Johnson Hall. From here, Van Buskirk and the Third New Jersey headed to Fort Ticonderoga, the massive fortification defending the southern end of Lake Champlain. At this post, joined to the rest of the Northern army, seeking to block the advancing British under Sir Guy Carleton. With the threatened invasion over and the establishment of the corps coming to an end, Van Buskirk returned to New Jersey and was discharged.

Van Buskirk's service was different than the experience of Harman Blauvelt, although both were Continentals for some time. When Van Buskirk entered the service, the maximum duration was but a year; Blauvelt, being a Levy, served only a few months alongside men who had enlisted for either three years or the duration of the war. Congress had eventually realized that short-term enlistments for the Continental army would not win the war. While living at Closter, he served in the Bergen County Militia, being captured on May 9, 1779, in a devastating raid on that town. One hundred men of the Fourth Battalion,

George Van Buskirk was one of only a handful of Bergen County residents to step up and enlist in the Continental army when the war broke out. Continental troops, such as these reenactors from the Second New Jersey Regiment, often faced shortages of proper uniforms but were the real backbone of Washington's army. *Courtesy of Susan Nabors Braisted.*

New Jersey Volunteers, under Captain Samuel Ryerson, ascended the Palisades from the Hudson and went through the village, taking cattle and prisoners, including Van Buskirk, who was bayoneted in the skirmishing during the raid. According to the Royal Gazette, *the Loyalists were in a particularly foul mood due to the treatment of Peter Myer, who had been killed the previous March (see Weart Banta).*

> Some time since Mr. Myers, an Ensign in a company of refugees, was killed in a skirmish with a party of rebels near Closter, the inhabitants of that place after his death, stripped his corps naked, hung him up by the neck, where he was exhibited as a public spectacle for many hours. The inhabitants of Closter have been remarkable for their persecution of, and cruelty to all the friends of government, and had fixed up in many of their houses advertisements, in which they expressed their determination of giving no quarter to refugees, and requested all Continental soldiers and militia to refuse them quarters.

After five months in the Sugar House prison, Van Buskirk was exchanged. His pension claim was initially filed under the 1818 act, which provided for destitute Continental army veterans.

Be it remembered that on this 2nd day of July 1830, personally appeared, in the Court of Common Pleas for the City and County of New York, in open court, being a court of record by the common law and by the statutes of the said state, George Van Buskirk, residing in the said city and county, who being first duly sworn according to law doth on his oath, make the following declaration in order to obtain the provision made by the acts of Congress of the 18th of March 1818, and the 1st of May 1820. That he the said George Van Buskirk is now aged seventy six years; That he enlisted on or about the beginning of the year 1776, for the term of one year, in the State of New Jersey, in the company commanded by Captain Anthony Sharp in the regiment commanded by Colonel Elias Dayton in the line of the State of New Jersey on the Continental establishment; that he continued to serve in said corps until some time in April in the following year when he was discharged at Morristown in the State of New Jersey; that after being discharged he enlisted as a volunteer and continued in the service until the 9th of May 1779, when he was taken prisoner by the British, at the burning of Closter and carried to the City of New York, and there

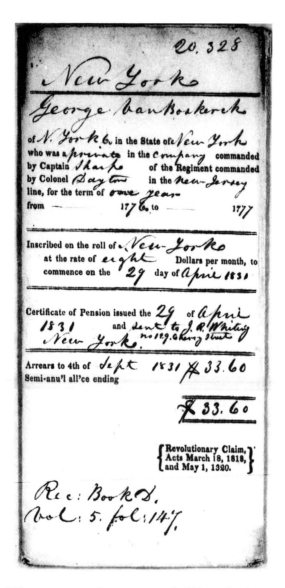

What every U.S. veteran wanted to see: approval of his application and a monetary reward for his services in the Revolution. *Courtesy of the National Archives and Records Administration, Washington, D.C.*

confined for upwards of five months when he was exchanged and received no regular discharge; that he hereby relinquishes every claim except the one presented the 11th of August 1818, and which was said to be returned to the Honorable R. Riker of New York on the 15th of April, 1819, in order to obtain proof of service; from that time to the present, he has not been able to obtain the declaration then presented though he has made repeated enquiries therefore, that he has made no other claim except the present; that his name is not on the roll of any state except the State of New Jersey.

CHAPTER 20

PETER S. VAN ORDEN

Hackensack Township

*T*his Hackensack Township militiaman led a remarkable career during the Revolution. His two family members on the opposite side of the conflict, John and William Van Orden, had both died by March 1778 while serving in the Fourth Battalion, New Jersey Volunteers. The object of our study here was much more fortunate, surviving well into the nineteenth century. Van Orden's family was from Schraalenburgh, the area of modern Bergenfield-Dumont-Haworth. Peter mentions that upon his return, he found his family's home completely plundered. This almost certainly occurred at the hands of Thomas Ward's Refugees, in one of their very first excursions from the post at Bull's Ferry, in the middle of June 1780. This was on the heels of a Refugee raid two weeks before on Closter. In that case, the orders issued by the commander of the Refugees had been "to seize, kill or apprehend the Rebel guards in that or any other part of the country you may march through, also every other disaffected person that is known to be aiding or assisting the Rebellion" but "not on any pretence whatever hurt or injure any of the well disposed loyal Inhabitants." The raid had devastated the town. Among the damage done was the destruction of the homes of Major John Maritius Goetschius and militiaman Derick Banta.

Van Orden had returned to Bergen County just in time to take part in the fighting at Fort Lee in May 1781. The three skirmishes at the site had left a half dozen militiamen wounded and perhaps a few killed. They, unknowingly, were being reinforced by four hundred Continental Light Infantry under Colonel Alexander Scammell, who had orders from Washington to drive off the Refugees. Logistics problems and a rainstorm delayed their appearance when it became evident the Refugees had abandoned the post. On May 23, 1781, the British had ordered Thomas Ward to give up his

The blockhouse started by the Refugees at Fort Lee in 1781 was never finished. The British, finding the Refugees "rather averse to fortifying themselves," ordered the post evacuated shortly after work commenced. The battles were commemorated with a weekend of living history at Fort Lee Historic Park in 2006. *Courtesy of Fort Lee Historic Park.*

plans for Fort Lee and establish a new post at Bergen Point (Bayonne). This would become Fort DeLancey, named for the British adjutant general Oliver DeLancey Jr., a Huguenot Loyalist.

Prior to this, the British had put in motion two thousand troops to attack Colonel Scammell's force, including Van Buskirk's battalion. The orders were countermanded when the Refugees withdrew. Before sailing off, Ward sent off two spies, Peter John and Gilbert Thew. On May 26, the latter returned and reported:

Gilbert Thew went from Fort Lee last Sunday up to Slaughter's Landing, where he heard, the Continental Troops between five & six hundred under the command of Colonel Campbell [Scammell] were on their march to attack Fort Lee. That last Tuesday they had advanced as far as Liberty Pole, about four miles from the fort. That they had collected all the militia they could get. On Wednesday they marched back to Tappan and remained there that day and Thursday, heard nothing of them since. They had no cannon with them that he could hear of.

Thus ended the Fort Lee Campaign of 1781.

Van Orden would end his military service as a guest of the British, being taken prisoner by the Refugees in 1782 while patrolling for "London Traders." This term referred to inhabitants who traded with the British in New York. It was rumored the Refugees themselves kept an extensive store of goods in their blockhouse, trading with the inhabitants of Bergen for food or other locally produced items. Van Orden's pension application is No. S11160.

On this 28th day of November 1832, personally appeared in open court before the judges of the Court of Common Pleas, now sitting at the court house in Clarkstown in said County *[of Rockland]*, Peter S. Van Orden, a resident of the town of Ramapo in the County of Rockland, and State of New York, aged sixty nine years, the fourteenth day of August last past agreeable to the family record, who being duly sworn according to law, doth on his oath make the following declaration, in order to obtain the benefit of the Act of Congress, passed June 7th 1832. That he entered the service of the United States, under the following named Officers and served as herein after stated.

That he resided in the Township of Hackensack, County of Bergen and State of New Jersey. That He entered the service of the United States in the first part of the month of April 1778, at Schraalenburgh, by enlisting in a company commanded by Captain *[Abraham]* Haring, in Colonel Theunis Dey's Regiment for one month, (in the monthly service) was stationed first at Closter, afterwards removed along the lines, from place to place as occasion seemed to require. In May of the same year, under Captain *[Joseph]* Board. In June or the first week in July following, under Captain John Huyler, then under Captain Peter Ward then under Captain Elias Romaine, all of which were monthly enlistments, in the aforesaid regiment of Colonel Theunis Dey. That, about the latter part of the month of September, in the same year, the British surprised and captured the greater part of Captain Romaine's Company, together with some standing troops then under the command of Lieutenant Barnes, who was also taken prisoner, with some of Captain *[John]* Bell's Company of 9 Months men. We then retreated to Harrington, when immediately afterwards, either on the last of September, or the first of October in said year of 1778, entered in the service of the

One of the prized items sought after by the War Office to verify service was the discharge. Militia, as well as state troops, rarely if ever received such a document. This discharge of Tan Sisco from Outwater's State Troops is a rare example. *Courtesy of the National Archives and Records Administration, Washington, D.C.*

United States, as a volunteer under Captain James Christie, remained at Harrington in company with a regiment of New York Militia under the command of *[Colonel]* Ann Hawkes Hay, and in company with a Corps of Horse commanded by Colonel *[George]* Baylor, until they were surprised by a party of British under command of General *[Charles]* Grey, as I then was informed, the most of Baylor's Corps were killed and taken, and also Captain Crane's Company of New York Militia, were killed and taken prisoners, and myself very narrowly escaped to Orangetown, in the State of New York, and joined the said company under Captain Christie at Clarkstown in the now County of Rockland. When the British Army retired to New York, Captain Christie and his company returned to Schraalenburgh and was discharged after one month's service.

On my return home, found the family stripped of almost every necessary of life and comfort, and the enemy still near them. I then removed with my mother's family into the now County of Rockland, procured a small situation for my mother and four fatherless children. Then enlisted again about the first of November in said year of 1778, in a company under command of Captain John Bell, of nine months men and was stationed at the house of Peter Van Houten in the now Town of Ramapo, County of Rockland under the command of Lieutenant Resolvert F. Van Houten until the latter part of the month of December then marched to Tappan; joined the company, and were discharged by the said Captain Bell on New Years Eve, on last day of December 1778. Then about the first of

April 1779, enlisted under command of Captain John Huyler, Colonel Dey's Regiment in Bergen County for one month, after said service was performed, was discharged, and then returned into the State of New York—did not perform any military duty to the best of my recollection only under Captain Henry Ternure on alarms, which were common in those trying days. Then in the first part in the month of July 1780, enlisted in a company commanded by Captain Jonathan Lawrence, in Colonel Lewis DuBois' Regiment at Clarkstown for three months, then went to Tappan and joined the company, at said place was engaged in erecting forts etc. for about the space of three weeks, then marched to King's Ferry, and embarked on board of vessels for Fishkill; was encamped about two weeks, from thence to Albany, Schenectady, after a short encampment then marched for Fort Plain, was detached with a small party to Fort Clyde to guard and protect the inhabitants of that place until some time in the month of October in the same year was then again ordered to Fort Plain when his said three months service expired. His officers then informed him of the awful and defenseless state of the inhabitants if the troops were discharged that *[Lieutenant Colonel Sir John]* Johnson and *[Chief Joseph]* Brant with British, Indians and Tories were on their way from Schoharie to that place, burning and destroying all before them, sparing neither age nor sex. The necessity of my country at the importunity of my officers, again induced me to render my services again to my country, induced me immediately to volunteer again, about the 20th of October. The regiment then, although not more than two hundred men or thereabouts and sixty Indians of the Oneida tribe marched down the river. Colonel *[John]* Brown with about two hundred men on our left, after marching about five or six miles, were attacked on the left. Colonel Brown with a number of his men were killed some taken, the remainder retreated to, or near Fort Plain, on the north side of the river close hemmed in by the enemy until late in the afternoon, was then reinforced by General *[Robert]* Van Rensselaer was joined with six hundred militia, *[Lieutenant]* Colonel *[Samuel]* Clyde with two hundred of his man joined Colonel DuBois' Regiment and marched in pursuit of the enemy, and overtook them about sunset. After some exchange of fire, was ordered to advance on the enemy, who gave way, we took one brass three pounder, some small arms, almost all their baggage, a great number of horses, and prisoners and redeemed our men that were prisoners in their possession. We remained on the field all night at break of day marched in pursuit of the enemy, forded the river and marched about twenty eight miles, hungry, wet, and weary; received about half a ration

During Peter S. Van Orden's absence from his native Schraalenburgh, the town had been raided by Thomas Ward's Loyal Refugee Volunteers in June 1780. Among the buildings burned was the home of Derick Banta. The house was rebuilt and today serves as Dumont's public library. *Courtesy of Todd W. Braisted.*

at Fort Herkimer that night and in the morning early marched in pursuit of the enemy in the wilderness, for about three days and a half without any sustenance except roots, then returned with the capture of only one Indian, met our provision almost night. The following day continued our march to Fort Herkimer. He was then ordered to the command a guard to take charge of the prisoners, returned to Schenectady, made a short stay, thence to Albany where we halted a week or more, then by water to Dutchess County and secured the prisoners in the common jail of said county, from thence marched to King's Ferry a heavy fall of snow overtook us on our march thence crossed the river into now Rockland County and were there discharged some time in the month of November, after about four months hard and tedious service. In April 1781 early in the month moved with my mother's family to Schraalenburgh in the Township of Hackensack, County of Bergen and State of New Jersey, his former place of residence. Immediately thereupon was enrolled in Captain James Christie's Company as a sergeant therein, in the regiment of Colonel Theunis Dey which regiment was immediately called into service.

The British, Refugees and Tories had taken possession of old Fort Lee and were busy repairing the same, not more than five or six miles from our station: we had skirmishes and engagements very frequently, until we dislodged the enemy, and drove them from the fort, with loss on both sides. After about one month's service, *[we]* were then discharged, which was about the first of the month of May, then immediately entered the service under Captain John Huyler, as a substitute for Daniel Peek, for one month which expired about the first of June, then entered as a substitute for Benjamin Westervelt, in a company commanded by Captain Peter Ward, for one month in the aforesaid regiment, then about the first of July he again volunteered under the aforesaid Captain Christie for one month, then again under the said Captain Christie he again volunteered for one month's service, which he thinks expired near the middle of the month of September, then again volunteered for one month under Captain John Huyler in said regiment, then under Captain Romaine for one month is not positive which of the two last mentioned services was first rendered, then again under Captain Christie for one month, which concludes and ends his services for 1781.

In 1782 entered volunteer service under Captain Christie, for one month, which service commenced about the first week in April.

Then under Captain John Huyler for same term of service, then under a Captain Board, for like term, then under Captain Christie for a like term, then under Captain Christie, and Major *[John Mauritius]* Goetschius for another like term of service, then again under the last named officers, for a like term of service, then some time in the month of October in the said year 1782, was sent by an order, from said Major Goetschius, as a sergeant, with a small party, as near the British out posts as practicable to intercept all trade and commerce, and prevent any intercourse with the enemy, when he was taken prisoner, carried to New York, & kept in confinement, until cessation of arms took place, was then released, the exact time of said imprisonment he is unable to state but thinks not exceeding one month.

His said within stated Revolutionary services from the commencement thereof, to the year 1781, was rendered as a private except about one month he thinks he served as a corporal, from thence to the close of the war chiefly as a Sergeant.

The black market, known in the Revolution as "London trading," provided a useful (though illegal) means for Bergen's inhabitants of all political stripes to trade their produce and livestock in exchange for British gold or imported goods from the markets in New York City. Militia patrols attempted to intercept such trade but seldom seriously curbed the practice. *Courtesy of Fort Lee Historic Park.*

He further states, that when the militia in the neighborhood of his residence were not called into actual service, the few remaining that were not killed, or imprisoned had to be continually on duty, at their own expense for the safety of the country and themselves. He does not recollect to have ever received a written discharge for any of his terms of service, nor does he remember of a written discharge given to any of the militia soldiers. All the proof he can offer, is the proof of some of those few yet remaining, that have served with him in the said Revolutionary War.

That when he first entered in service of the United States, which was at the age of between fourteen and fifteen years, he resided in the Township of Hackensack, County of Bergen, State of New Jersey, in the neighborhood of Schraalenburgh which was afterwards burned by the British, then removed to Clarkstown, in the County of Rockland, then again to Schraalenburgh, his first and former place of residence, from thence to the now Town of Clarkstown in Rockland County from thence to the Town of Hampstead in said county, now Ramapo, where he now resides.

And he verily believes that his whole term of service actually, honestly and faithfully rendered to his country, during the War of the Revolution, under the different services herein mentioned would amount at least in his belief to two years and six months.

He also hereby relinquishes every claim whatever to a pension or annuity, except the present, and hereby declares that his name is not on the Pension Roll of the agency of any state.

CHAPTER 21

RICHARD AND ELIZABETH WANNAMAKER

Ramapo

*T*he *Wannamaker family of Ramapo was one of Bergen's staunchly Loyalist families. Contributing no less than six members to Captain Peter Rutan's Company of the Fourth Battalion, New Jersey Volunteers; two others were members of John Bayard's King's Orange Rangers. The family members were certainly unlucky in their military careers. Henry, Peter, John and Nicholas Wannamaker were all taken prisoner less than two weeks into their service, being amongst sixteen men of the Fourth Battalion who were taken prisoner in Bergen Woods by a large force under Continental generals Parsons and Clinton. They would remain prisoners until their exchange on October 2, 1778, when upon their return, they found another family member in the battalion, Conrad Wannamaker, had died of smallpox the previous March.*

The subject of this profile was the sixth family member to serve, Richard (or Dirck) Wannamaker. Richard, like the other members of his family, served in Captain Rutan's Company, enlisting on December 7, 1776. Unlike his relatives, this Wannamaker served without incident in the battalion until early in the morning of August 19, 1779. A few hours previously, the bulk of the battalion, personally commanded by Lieutenant Colonel Abraham Van Buskirk, had marched from their post at Paulus Hook to English Neighborhood to search for a party of U.S. troops said to be there. In fact, the enemy Van Buskirk was in quest of was a force of some four hundred Continental troops on their way to attack Paulus Hook. Remaining behind at the post was a mixed force of less than two hundred men made up primarily of the Garrison Battalion (old or invalid soldiers), a few Hessians and about sixty New Jersey Volunteers, one of whom was

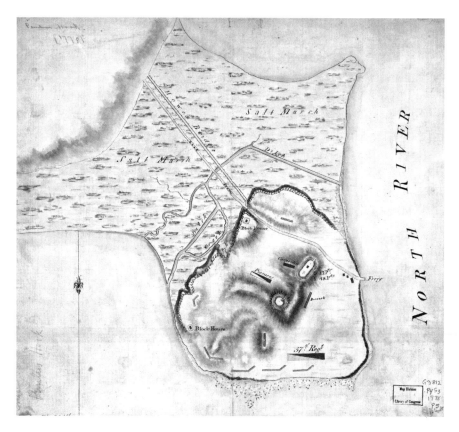

Paulus Hook had been captured by the British in September 1776, two months before the fall of Fort Lee to the north. It would remain a British fort through the end of the war. *Courtesy of the Library of Congress, Washington, D.C.*

Richard Wannamaker. The ensuing assault was described by the New-York Gazette and the Weekly Mercury:

> *That nearly about half an hour after two, the Rebels in three divisions (exceeding 400 men) passed the ditch in front of the abbatis, about 20 yards from the abbatis, where they were fired upon by a few sentries, but having seized immediately on the block-house guards (who in place of defending their post, ran out to see what was the matter) they proceeded to the works, which they soon became masters of, with the cannon, etc. But they were so confused, and alarmed, they neither spiked the cannon, nor damaged the barracks, or made any other use of their victory, than carrying off about 100 prisoners, among whom are ten Hessians (whose loss is much regretted) and four officers of Colonel Buskirk's Battalion, and plundering a few women.*

The prisoners from Paulus Hook were marched to Philadelphia, where they were placed in the "New Jail." Conditions in the jail, like all prisons of the time, were unpleasant at best. Eight of the New Jersey Volunteers taken at Paulus Hook died between the end of March and beginning of June 1780, one of whom was Richard Wannamaker. His widow, Elizabeth, was left to carry on within the British lines. Her predicament of losing her husband in the service was sadly all too common. It is entirely possible she was not even aware of his passing until the general exchange of prisoners in May and June 1783, when any not returning at that point were struck from the rolls. There were no official means to convey news of this sort, with family members having to rely on the word of comrades who were exchanged or escaped and returned to their corps. It is not unusual that she remarried to another soldier in the battalion; the unit being her extended family during the time of her husband's imprisonment, she would have necessarily developed relationships within the battalion, if for no other reason than necessity. Her losses were typical of a small farm in Bergen County at the time.

The memorial of Elizabeth Wannamaker, formerly of Bergen County New Jersey, and now a settler at Fredericton, in New Brunswick most humbly sheweth

That her husband was Richard Wannamaker, one of the King's loyal subjects in New Jersey, and being persecuted by the Rebels he came within the British lines in the year 1776, having before he made his escape from the enemy engaged to serve in the New Corps. That agreeable to such engagement he joined the army, and was taken a prisoner in the year 1779, and by hard usage died a prisoner in Philadelphia Jail in the year 1780.

That the Rebels seized upon and confiscated the property of her said husband, and thereby deprived your memorialist of the means of subsisting in that country, and reduced her to the necessity of coming to this country.

That the annexed is a state of her losses, which she is ready to prove with the necessary evidence when indulged with a hearing.

Wherefore your memorialist requests she may be examined when the Honorable the Commissioners arrive in this province, and such relief may be granted as her losses merit, and as in duty bound she will ever pray.

[Losses]
A tract of land in Ramapo,
   Bergen County, New Jersey
   worth in the year 1775   £ 187. 10. 0.

House & other improvements,
6 milk cows, 3 horses, a number of sheep,
hogs, heifers, calves etc.   £ 100.   0. 0.

[Total] Halifax Currency   £ 287. 10. 0.

Evidence on the claim of Elizabeth Wannamaker, late of New Jersey.

Claimant Sworn:

Says she came from New York in September 1783, & has lived at Fredericton on the back part of Maugerville ever since.

She is a native of New Jersey. Her late husband, Richard Wannamaker was always a loyal man & joined the British Army in 1776, at New York. He had never joined the Rebels.

He was taken at Paulus Hook & carried to Philadelphia Jail, where he died. He was then a soldier in *[Lieutenant]* Colonel Buskirk's Regiment. He left no will, nor any child. He left *[a]* brother and sister in New Jersey.

Claimant married John Post, a sergeant in Colonel Buskirk's Regiment who came here in 1783, and is now settled in Maugerville.

100 acres in Bergen County, the property of her late husband. He had it from his father. There was a house & most of it cleared. It is valued at £3 Currency per acre. Says that the Rebels seized this at her husband's death. Had 6 cows, 3 horses, 5 or 6 sheep, and some young cattle, all taken by the Rebels. She has sent for a Certificate of Sale.

CHAPTER 22

JOHN ZABRISKIE

New Bridge

*J*ohn *Zabriskie is one of the better-known Loyalists of Bergen County today, even if people are not entirely aware of why. Zabriskie's lasting monument today, and well-detailed below, is his beautiful home that is the centerpiece of Historic New Bridge Landing, the home of the Bergen County Historical Society. Located on the west bank of the Hackensack River, Zabriskie's house and mill sat astride the strategic crossing point of the Hackensack River, the waterway that combined with the Hudson to form Bergen Neck out of much of the county's land. While Zabriskie's claim is sparse on details of his service (it was filed in London by an attorney while the claimant himself was in Nova Scotia), it provides a wealth of information on his property, highly useful to historians today in preserving and interpreting this great historic site. In early 1781, Zabriskie himself was given a captain's commission in the Guides & Pioneers, the corps commanded by Major John Aldington of English Neighborhood. Little is known of what Zabriskie's actual duties were after joining the British, although it most likely involved gathering intelligence, as exemplified in this September 25, 1780 letter from the mayor of New York City, David Mathews: "Mr. Zabriskie came to town this morning and is at Mr. Godlet's in Hanover Square. He is able to give you some intelligence relative to the present situation of the Rebel army and the confusion that prevails amongst them. He informs me that from what he could learn Major André would be safe. I hope to God it may be true. I wish you would call on Zabriskie as he wishes to keep house for some days."*

With his property confiscated, John Zabriskie left for a new life in Nova Scotia. While the normal process would have been for the state to sell the confiscated property at public auction, in this instance, Zabriskie's home was given as a present to the drill master of the Continental army, the Prussian-born major general Baron von Steuben. His claim is filed in the TNA's AO 13/95/490-494.

The memorial of Charles Cooke as attorney to and in behalf of John Zabriskie a half pay captain in the British American Forces very respectfully sheweth

That in the month of January 1784 the said Zabriskie empowered William Bayard Esqr. to lodge his claim agreeable to Act of Parliament for his property confiscated, as will appear by the enclosed powers.

That the said William Bayard being informed that claimants would not be permitted to substantiate this claim by attorneys, but be obliged either to relinquish their said claims or appear before the commissioners in person, and knowing that the said John Zabriskie's circumstances were so deranged by the confiscation of his property that he had not either resources of money or credit sufficient to enable him to come to this country to prosecute his claim, therefore the said William Bayard neglected to lodge the claim of the said John Zabriskie conformable to the aforementioned Act of Parliament.

That the said John Zabriskie can produce unquestionable testimony of his early disinterested and persevering acts of loyalty, the proscription of his person and confiscation of his valuable property, in consequence thereof which has reduced him to penury.

Your Memorialist therefore in behalf of the said John Zabriskie, does very respectfully pray, that as it was owing to the negligence of William Bayard Esqr. and not the fault of the said John Zabriskie that his claim has not been lodged, conformable to Act of Parliament, that you may be pleased to recommend the name of the said John Zabriskie to be inserted in the next Act of Parliament appointing commissioners, in order that he may be permitted to come forward in support of said claim, or such other relief as you may be pleased to extend to him. And your memorialist shall pray etc.

An account and estimate of the real estate of John Zabriskie late of the County of Bergen in New Jersey, but now a refugee in the City of New York, and which has been confiscated by virtue of a law of the Assembly of the State of New Jersey & is now possessed under the said Confiscation Law to wit.

John Zabriskie's mansion house today is the centerpiece of Historic New Bridge Landing. Confiscated by the state for Zabriskie's loyalty to the British, the house was given as a gift to one of Washington's generals, Baron von Steuben. *Courtesy of Deborah Powell.*

One large mansion house seventy feet long & forty feet wide containing twelve rooms built with stone, with the outhouses consisting of a bake house, smoke house, coach house, & two large barns, and a garden situate at a place called New Bridge, on the River Hackensack three miles from the court house in Hackensack being the County Town estimated & valued at £850. 0. 0.

One large grist mill containing two pair of stones adjoining the said mansion house 1200. 0. 0.

Forty acres of land adjoining the said mansion house consisting of meadow land & two orchards @ £25 per acre 1000. 0. 0.

163

Seventy acres of wood land & arable land lying half a mile from the said mansion house on the East side of Hackensack River @ £11. 15. per acre	812.	10.	0.
One other tract of fifteen Acres of wood land lying about two miles from the said mansion house @ £10. per acre	150.	0.	0.
One other tract of arable of wood land containing one hundred & fifty one acres & half an acre of land lying at Pascack, about six miles from the said New Bridge @ £5. 15. per acre	871.	2.	6.
One other tract of salt meadow containing 60 acres @ £6. 0. 0.	360.	0.	0.
Current money of New York	£5243. 12.		6.

Be it remembered that on the eleventh day of October in the year of our Lord One Thousand Seven Hundred & Eighty Three Joost Zabriskie farmer, John Van Norden miller, and Samuel Demarest farmer all of Bergen County in New Jersey, appeared before me David Mathews Esquire Mayor of the said City of New York who being duly sworn, jointly & severally depose & say, that they have long lived in the neighborhood of the estate of John Zabriskie at New Bridge in Bergen County aforesaid and that they are & have long been well acquainted with the mansion house, out houses, mill, & the several tracts of land contained in the within estimate, and that from the knowledge they have of their real value, they have appraised & valued them at the several rates of sums affixed to each of them, which they verily believe are not estimated over but under the true & real value thereof.

And these deponents further severally say that when the said John Zabriskie fled from New Jersey to New York in the year 1780, he owned & was possessed of all the houses & tracts of land contained in the said estimate in his own right, and they further depose & say that since the said John Zabriskie fled within the King's Lines at New York as aforesaid all his estate in the said County of Bergen has been confiscated pursuant to an Act of the Assembly of New Jersey, and that his said mansion house, mill & the several tracts of land contained in the said foregoing estimate are now possessed by persons who hold the same under the Commissioners for Confiscated Estates in the said County of Bergen & further say not.

Sworn before me the
day & year above written
> David Mathews

Epilogue

The Revolution's Bergen County veterans left a legacy that is still felt and seen today well beyond the borders of the county. Those who remained loyal to the British helped settle and expand modern Canada, giving it ties to New Jersey probably little considered at the time. The same unique culture that made up Bergen County in 1776 by extension was then transferred to places like Shelburne, Maugerville, Saint John and Fredericton. By the same token, those from Bergen who fought for and helped found the new United States often picked up the new spirit of exploration and travel, spreading throughout the ever expanding borders of the country, adding the names of Hackensack Valley families into new territories and distant settlements.

As the years passed, and the survivors dwindled in number, they took on an almost new sense of celebrity, particularly as the United States neared impending civil war. One of those celebrated was veteran Peter Van Buskirk. Van Buskirk's actual service in the American Revolution was extremely limited, acting as a "forage master" at the age of nineteen, when the war was in its end stages. He spent far more years convincing the War Department in the Nineteenth Century that his service actually occurred, and that it was worth a pension, and in an amount equal to that of a low ranking officer. As it turned out, he had plenty of time to find evidence and press his claim. And he was successful. Among the many papers in his pension application was one docketed "Extract From the 'Passaic Guardian' published at Paterson N.J." It gives quite a remarkable account of perhaps Bergen County's last living veteran from the Revolution.

"Peter Van Buskirk of Washington, is ninety-nine years old. He was on the Revolutionary pension, but as a private. As such he had received $8 a month. But he claimed to have been assistant forage master, and he recently found evidence to establish his claim. He is therefore awarded arrearages to the amount of $16,200."

The above from a New York paper refers to Mr. Peter Van Buskirk of Bergen County, where some of his children, more grandchildren, and numerous great grand children and great great grand children still reside, principally in the neighborhood of Saddle River. With the exception of a siege of fever and ague since living in Washington, Mr. Van Buskirk has never had any sickness worth mentioning, and his eyesight is still unimpaired, rendering the use of glasses unnecessary. He has always avoided the use of tobacco, ardent spirits and even tea and coffee, and to his temperate habits may, in a great measure be attributed his good health and remarkable longevity. As a somewhat curious fact it may be stated that a couple years ago he told our informant that for the last seven years he had partaken of no drink whatever not even so much as a glass of water.

In politics Mr. Van Buskirk is a Republican, and his vote has always been given for these principles of Liberty and Union for which he labored in his youth, during the soul-trying period of the Revolution.

The first part of the above was apparently published in the July 12, 1861 edition of the New York Times, *which itself was re-publishing an article from the* Washington Star *of July 10. That article reads in full:*

For some years past PETER VAN BUSKIRK, of this city, aged 99 years, who has been upon the revolutionary pension rolls as a private, at $5 per month, for many years, has been prosecuting a claim for arrearages of pension as an Assistant Forage-Master, which, if allowed, entitled him to receive a total pension of $50 per month, instead of $5, the amount heretofore paid to him. His claim was more than once rejected for want of testimony. Recently he has found and presented the necessary testimony, and yesterday his claim was duly allowed, with an award of $16,200 back (arrearages of) pension. This is, we believe, the largest back pension ever obtained from the Treasury of the United States. The officers of the bureau, though believing him entitled to be placed on the roll as an. Assistant Forage-Master, could not previously allow his claim for want of the requisite legal evidence to substantiate it.

The reminders of the war remain with us today. Here, modern veterans in River Vale salute the dead of the Third Light Dragoons killed in 1778. The remains were discovered in 1967, in what is now Baylor Park. *Courtesy of Janet E. Strom.*

In August 1861, Peter Van Buskirk's niece, seventy-seven-year-old Lucy Hopper, remarked to the War Department testimony similar to that which could have been given by countless other offspring from the veterans:

That her said Uncle [*Peter Van Buskirk*] if alive must be about 99 or 100 years of age. That his Grand Father (old Uncle Abraham) whom she well recollects lived until he was 99. That she has always heard her Grandmother Van Buskirk say that her children were born about two years apart, and she used often to say that she awaited until her two years were up before she had another baby. That she, deponent, lived in New Jersey until after the War of 1812, when she came to this city [*New York*] and has lived here ever since. That she well recollects the death of her Grand Father Thomas Van Buskirk, who fell in the fire in a fit and was burned to death. That deponent then lived in Hoppertown, near her Grand Father's residence. That she recollects her father's relating his service in the Revolution and also recollects distinctly the frequent conversations had between her said father and her Uncle Peter in regard to said services. That her father had a beautiful book of maps

The broken, worn grave marker of a Revolutionary War veteran at Old North Church, Dumont. *Courtesy of Todd W. Braisted.*

of the battles of the Revolution, and the officer's names therein. That she frequently heard him say what a large man General Greene was, and that when in the war, that bullets would whistle around his head, until he did not know whether he had a hat on or not, and they would frequently converse about her Uncle Peter's buying grain for the army who laid near the house of her grand father and that when her father and her Uncle Peter would be out, her grandmother was in great dread of the British. That her grandmother had a large leather bag into which she would put her silver and put the bag above the closet in a hole. That upon one occasion the British came to their house and even lifted up the flag stones in the cellar in search of valuables and that she could relate numerous incidents in regard to the war from their conversations…

North of the border, the Bergen County veterans living in British North America had their own similar issues to deal with. On March 23, 1839, the New Brunswick House of Assembly granted their Revolutionary War veterans relief, in the form of "An Act for the relief of old Soldiers of the Revolutionary War and their Widows." The act would allow veterans in "indigent or distressed circumstances," as well as their widows, residing within the province to apply for annual pensions of ten pounds. Among those applying would be Peter Allen, formerly of Hackensack. He was one of three brothers of his family who enlisted shortly after the battalion established its post at Hoebuck in 1779. He filed a claim for a pension, which in part read:

That he was a private soldier in the 4th Battalion of the New Jersey Volunteers commanded by Lieutenant Colonel Buskirk. That he served in the said regiment seven years, was wounded in an engagement at a place called the burnt meadows on Staten Island.

That he came to the Province of New Brunswick in 1783, lost his discharge in a house that was consumed by fire. That he never received any land from the Crown, he is now in the seventy sixth year of his age, in very indigent circumstances, and unable to labor as he was want to do.

As modest as the support offered by the province may have been, it was an essential monetary lifeline for aged veterans and, increasingly as the years passed by, the widows they left behind. By all accounts, the government, through the bureaucracy and the banks, administered the payments flawlessly. Well, almost flawlessly. In 1859 in the Town of St. Stephen, on the border with Maine, an unidentified government functionary forgot or by some other lapse was several times neglectful of his duty in processing the proper paperwork for paying the widows. These ladies, many of whom had been followers of the army, and nearly all destitute refugees from the new United States, had survived hardship and deprivation before and now were not about to let some government bureaucrat cause them additional want and misery. Knowing the pen to be mightier than the sword, the widows unleashed one written volley after another in the direction of government, directing their wrath upon the hapless "Commissariat Useless." Here then is the scene of battle from 1859:

To,
His Excellency
The Lieut. Governor etc. etc. etc.

Sir,

The pensioners residing within 15 miles of Saint Stephen, in the County of Charlotte, attended at the bank this day, expecting to receive their pension in accordance with the regulations of the War Office, but were told by Robert Watson Esqr. the cashier who pays the pensioners at this place, that the commissariat had not sent the papers authorizing the payment, and consequently he could not let us have our money.

We are satisfied that the Secretary at War would not permit the commissariat to retain office one day were we to bring our complaint under his notice. And we entertain the same opinion of your Excellency and most respectfully ask your interference.

Your Excellency's

most obedient humble servants

The Pensioners at St. Stephen

St. Stephen
County of Charlotte
October 1ˢᵗ 1859.

P.S.

This is the fifth time we have had cause of complaint against this commissariat who has we presume got into office through some palpable mistake, and we hope there will be neither delay or mistake in turning him out of office forthwith.

[at bottom of letter]

we are too poor to put this our complaint in an envelope

[addressed on reverse]

On Her Majesty's Service

To His Excellency
    The Lieutenant Governor and
        Commander in Chief
            etc etc etc
                Fredericton

[Included was a debit note prepared by the widows.]

1859 Mr. Commissariat Useless

To Pensioners at St. Stephen Dr.

To formerly & fraudulently detaining our pension in violation of the Regulations of the War Office	£1.	5.	0.
Continued dereliction and neglect	1.	5.	0.
amount due	£2.	10.	0.

If your Excellency will have the goodness to have the above amount deducted from the pay of Mr. Commissariat Useless and sent to us pensioners it will be an Act of Justice to us and a benefit to Mr. Useless as it may rouse him from his lethargy and restore him to usefulness viz. if he ever was good for anything.

P.S.

Please send the amount to Robert Watson Esqr. He is cashier at St. Stephens Bank and will hand it over <u>instantly</u>.

There was no further account of Commissariat Useless, or any additional missed pension payments. On both sides of the border, the war had been remembered.

SOURCES

A few words on the sources of research used in the production of this text are in order. The pension applications for those soldiers of the United States are found in the National Archives and Records Administration (NARA) in Washington, D.C., while the Loyalist claims for compensation are found in the Audit Office (or AO) Papers of The National Archives (TNA) of the United Kingdom, located in Kew, Richmond, Surrey. Other records at TNA that were extremely helpful include the Colonial Office, Class 5 Papers, and that of Treasury, Class 1.

Many other primary sources have been used in verifying and adding to the text concerning all the applications. Of particular use was the Sir Henry Clinton Papers at the University of Michigan's William L. Clements Library in Ann Arbor and the George Washington Papers in the Library of Congress in Washington, D.C. Further information was substantiated through muster rolls, those for the United States as part of NARA's M246 Revolutionary War Rolls and in Ottawa at Library and Archives Canada's RG 8, "C" Series of Military Records.

As today, activities of the times were often recorded in the press. New York City published three newspapers during the British occupation, the *Royal Gazette*, the *Royal American Gazette* and the *New-York Gazette and the Weekly Mercury* while New Jersey eventually published two, which were, of course, pro-United States: the *New Jersey Gazette* in Burlington/Trenton and the *New Jersey Journal* in Chatham. All carried reports of the day, mostly gleaned through official reports and open letters.

The beautiful Georgian mansion of Colonel Theunis Dey, commander of the Bergen County Militia. Located now in the town of Wayne, it is owned and operated by the County of Passaic. *Courtesy of Library of Congress.*

For more information on the American Revolution in Bergen County, please visit www.bergencountyhistory.org.

INDEX

Y

Z

ABOUT THE AUTHOR

Todd W. Braisted is a past president of the Bergen County Historical Society, an honorary vice-president of the United Empire Loyalist Association of Canada and a Fellow of the Company of Military Historians. He has co-authored several books on the American Revolution, as well as numerous published journal articles. Todd has appeared as a guest historian on PBS's *History Detectives* and the CBC's *Who Do You Think You Are?* He has lectured extensively on Loyalists and the American Revolution throughout the United States and Canada. Todd is a resident of Mahwah, New Jersey, where he lives with his wife, Susan.

Visit us at
www.historypress.net